Reviews from the first edition

"As an incoming MBA student with a non-tr
book was incredibly informative. Stephen la
landscape - from the summer before your first year of school, through
the intense recruiting process, all the way through the (hopeful) offer
signing process. The book answered all of my questions - even ones that
I didn't know I had. The book is straightforward, honest, and written
from someone who really knows what he is talking about (Stephen went
through the process himself, landed a job at McKinsey, worked on the
recruiting side of McKinsey, and now works for Tuck helping to prep
students for this process). A must read for rising MBA students
interested in entering the consulting profession"

"A transition is never easy, let alone jumping from academic bench
science into management consulting. I have a life sciences background,
currently a PhD candidate in Microbiology & Immunology. I had the
fortune of reading this book by Stephen Pidgeon, and found it
extremely helpful in designing, paving, and walking the path in seeking a
career in management consulting. I greatly appreciated his wisdom and
advice in preparatory work and networking, but also in revealing the
industry to an inexperienced academic like myself."

"I would recommend this easy, helpful read for anyone - not just MBAs -
seeking/considering a career in management consulting. Knowing is half
the battle, and this book certainly does the trick"

"The book provides excellent advice to students trying to successfully
navigate consulting recruiting, and reading it was like getting a private
session from a knowledgeable coach."

"How To Get A Job in Consulting was a constant reference for me during
my summer internship search and took a lot of mystery out of the
process."

"Absolutely loved the book. As someone just beginning to explore the
consulting field, this is a great starting point. Stephen does a great job of

structuring the book. He begins by demystifying what it actually means to be a consultant (which in my opinion is the most important part of the book). Then, he takes the reader into the shoes of the recruiter and the consultants/partners helping in the recruiting process. This is extremely valuable because it allows you to enter the recruiting process with a consultant's mindset. By this, I mean that you are able to view the firm you are applying to as a "client" so to speak. This will give you a huge leg up on the competition. While others are stressing about parts of the interview process that don't matter, you come in to the recruiting process with a plan, ready to execute. This is your go to book for getting all things consulting. Before confusing yourself on company websites, read this book first to help you understand how to get where you want to be.

"There's so much emphasis everywhere on case practice, but this book goes way beyond that – it gave me the insider's guide to what the consulting recruiting process is really about."

"I'm an undergrad, and I've used a lot of the other consulting prep resources. Stephen's advice has been the most useful by far."

"Contains actionable tips and strategies to improve not only interview performance, but all of the other elements that go into the consulting recruiting process. Very useful."

"I would highly recommend the book as you seek to get your foot in the door: it is very easy to read and includes practical recommendations on what works and what doesn't."

"One of the greatest thing this book does is depicting to you a vivid picture of what consulting is, what consultant's life looks like, how consultants think, and how recruiters/inverviewers think, which is very useful for outsiders trying to understand consulting life and the recruiting process."

"This is a clear, concise book (in contrast to several other titles on the topic) that provides all the essential information on how to get a job in consulting. I finished it in only a few days and learned a ton. This book is especially valuable for folks with limited understanding of how consulting firms recruit. Highly recommend!"

"As the Director of the MBA Career Centre at Rotman, a career coach, and a former management consultant, I couldn't rate this book more highly. Stephen has really spelled it ALL out. Read this book, put it into practice, work with your coach, and you are one step closer to your dream job. Thanks Stephen - this was missing in the marketplace"

"I recently went through the consulting recruiting process, and I would definitely recommend this book to others. Stephen provides great insight into each stage of the recruiting process, from the networking receptions to the final round interviews, and does so in a way that is fun and easy-to-read. Stephen is very detail oriented and provides thoughtful advice on how every candidate can genuinely make a strong impression while being honest with him or herself. His unique perspective as a former McKinsey consultant and career advisor allows him to shed light onto many of the unique nuances of the recruiting process. I'd highly recommend this to anyone who is even considering a career in consulting."

"I used this book as part of my (successful) consulting recruiting recently. Coming from a non traditional business background, this was an incredibly helpful tool in orienting myself to the process of getting through the recruiting experience in a logical way. It really helped me understand what being a consultant is all about and how the structure of interviews actually reflects this - and, building on this, a clear guide to the actions that I could take to be successful."

HOW TO GET A JOB IN CONSULTING

Second edition

By Stephen Pidgeon

Acknowledgements

No book is the work of only one person, and I'd like to thank everyone whose input and encouragement made this possible.

For the many interviews that guided the book as it took shape, I'd like to thank everyone who agreed to give their valuable time and insights.

For editing, special thanks to Ron, Penny and Danielle.

Thanks to Jonathan, Gina, Steve, Matt and everyone at Tuck for supporting my writing endeavors and helping spread the word to a wide audience, and thanks to my many colleagues in career offices around the world for your input and help – I hope this edition will continue to be just as useful as the last one.

Thanks to my friends and colleagues at McKinsey for teaching me so much not only about the content of this book but also about how to follow my energy. I loved working with you and I love vicariously sharing your adventures.

Thanks to Caroline for sharing your writing experiences and making me feel like a writer myself, to Kevin for accompanying me on so many amazing writing journeys, to the many students and readers who have given me so much valuable feedback.

All opinions, and mistakes, are mine.

Contents

Introduction

What is this book about?

The goal of this book is to help you get a job with a top management consulting company. Its primary audience is current and prospective business students (MBA or undergrad), although it should also be very useful to anyone going through one of the other channels into consulting, including experienced hires.

Before we begin, let's cover some questions that may be on your mind:

- Why should you listen to me (or buy this book)?
- Don't you just need to get good at cases?
- Let's say you're heading off to business school – won't you get all this information once you arrive?

Why should you listen to me (or buy this book)?

I believe I'm in a fairly unique situation that gives me a lot of insight into consulting recruiting. I've been through it as a student, a consultant, and now a career coach at a top business school.

First, I went through this as an MBA student. In the summer of 2005 I arrived at the Tuck School of Business with the aim of taking two years to think about my future. I knew that when I left business school I'd have to earn some serious money, in order to pay off the loans I'd just signed. I also knew, from reading Bloomberg Business Week and various websites, that there was something called consulting that sounded interesting. Shortly after I arrived, I found myself attending presentations from companies, talking to consultants at networking events, then visiting their offices.

A couple of months after that I was drafting my cover letter and applying for summer internships. I was also practicing case interviews and rehearsing my 'fit' stories. In January, I interviewed with a number of companies and received a number of offers.

I chose to join McKinsey & Company, first as a Summer Associate, and then as a full time Associate when I graduated.

At McKinsey, I sat on the other side of the table – now I was a consultant who chose to get involved in interviewing and recruiting activities. I attended recruiting events at universities, spoke at presentations, met students at networking events, and made recommendations on who to interview. After a year as a consultant I was interviewer trained, and from then on I frequently gave interviews to candidates. In my first year of this I was restricted to first round interviews, and then as I became a more experienced consultant and interviewer, I was allowed to do decision-round interviews, and take part in the final decision meeting.

I worked at McKinsey for about four years. I started as an Associate, and then got promoted to Engagement Manager. I started to specialize in healthcare work, and I also developed a functional specialty in 'org' work. I made some great friends, and had some amazing experiences.

When I got the opportunity to return to Tuck, to work in career services, I jumped at the chance.

Now I work in the Career Development Office (CDO) at Tuck (one of the world's top business schools) where it's my job to counsel MBA and undergraduate students and help them get their dream consulting job. Each year I provide personal counseling and coaching to several hundred students who are trying to get a job in consulting. Many of the students I've counseled are now working at top consulting companies, or are headed there soon.

I also work closely with recruiters to help them achieve their goal of hiring the best candidates. Part of my job is to understand the nuances between firms, and to keep abreast of how each firm runs its recruiting and interviewing process. I do this by maintaining close relationships with both senior consultants and recruiting staff at each firm and regularly talking with them about these issues.

To summarize, I have a good perspective on the process of recruiting, and I've been able to hone my opinions regarding what works and what doesn't work over many hundreds of coaching sessions.

Don't you just need to get good at cases?

One of the primary interview methods used by consulting companies is the case interview. If you are going to interview for a consulting job, you will need to learn this new skill.

What I experienced when I was a student, and what I see now, is that there is an incredible depth of advice for students on the tactical issue of succeeding in a case interview.

This is not a case interview book. There are lots of those already, and if you are interested in getting a job with a consulting company you need to buy one. In fact, I've written one (which of course I highly suggest!) called 'Case Interviews For Beginners.'

However, one of the biggest problems I have seen is that students put all of their energy into case preparation, to the detriment of the other aspects such as networking or preparing for the fit interview. It's a natural reaction. The case is an exotic new skill, and it looms in the future like a scary obstacle course. People who are interested in consulting are usually clever, they usually like doing puzzles, and they have often achieved success in their lives by studying hard, nailing a new skill, and translating that mix of ability and practice into a successful performance.

Getting a consulting job, however, is about so much more than 'doing' a good case.

Think of a race car driver (think Nascar or Formula One, whichever is your preference). Someone setting out to be a world class race driver would first have to master the skill of driving the car. That's like learning how to do a case interview. You can't compete without this basic competence. But everybody who can drive a car is not going to win a world class race. When (insert your favorite driver's name here) is hurtling around the track, do you think he is thinking about whether to look in the mirror, or how heavily to put his foot down on the accelerator? No – that stuff is automatic, and has been for years. Now he's thinking about the art of the race – what his opponents are doing, what the weather is doing, how close to the edge he can take his car, you get the idea.

Every year I see students going into consulting interviews who are, in the terms of analogy above, newly qualified drivers. They have worked hard, and have reached the point where they are satisfied with their ability to operate the car, but that's all they can do. They walk into the interview room with a grim determination to 'ace the case', and drive competently around the track. However, the interviewer is seeing 10 people that day, and the company is seeing a couple of thousand in that season, and they only want to hire, let's say, 50. You can be sure they're not looking for people who can safely navigate around the track. They're looking for the next World Champion.

My goal with this book is that you can understand the difference between someone who can competently do a case interview, and the person who will get the job. If you can understand that, then I believe you'll have the best starting point as you head into recruiting season.

Let's say you're heading off to business school – won't you get all this information once you arrive?

As I sit writing this book, a typical reader I have in mind is a student who this August will arrive at business school. There's so much I want to tell you, prospective MBA, and as I sit in my office in Spring there is plenty of time to tell it to you. But when you get here, you'll be so busy it will make you ill (literally).

Don't believe me? Here's a representative view of what the first six weeks at a top business school is like:

Week one: Orientation

Every day you will have a dizzying number of parties, welcome events, practical logistical events (getting your ID card, your parking permit, etc.) and intro classes.

You will meet your new study group – four or five classmates who you will grow to simultaneously love and hate, as you will spend many hours together every day for the coming term, working as a team on every piece of work for every class.

You will try to make the most of your surroundings. At Tuck for instance you will get out into the mountains, onto the river, you'll sample local restaurants and pubs.

If you are living off-campus, you'll try to get to a furniture store to replace what you couldn't bring with you. You might even need to go out and buy a car and major appliances. Ordinarily these are things that you'd spend many weeks researching online. Now you'll have to conduct your research, get to the store or browse the websites, and conclude the purchase in a thirty minute window between a class and the start of your study group session.

Week two: Classes Start

Classes. This is what you're here for, right? Each class will require extensive pre-work, which will require extensive late night study group sessions. Each night you'll get to the point where you have to sleep, so you'll promise yourself and your study group that you'll get up early tomorrow to finish the reading, or the required analysis.

Careers. You'll come and meet with your Career Development advisor. We'll talk about your goals. I'll explain how our office works. I'll show you how to navigate some of our technology. You'll nod, excited about all of the opportunities ahead of you, but ten minutes after our meeting you'll have forgotten what we talked about (I'm not criticizing, I understand, you're busy, and you've got a lot on your mind).

Clubs. You'll attend the club fair and sign up for basketball club , consulting club, general management club (in case consulting doesn't work out), finance club (you're curious about the money those guys earn), the wine club (why not enjoy the good life while you're here!) and so on. Each club you sign up for will take up three or four hours of your time per week, every week, minimum.

Social life. Maybe you came here with your partner? Maybe you've come here looking for a partner?! Either way, you want to give yourself time with that person, or trying to find that potential person.

Week Three. Consulting club.

This is what you're here for, right? The consulting club is run by second years who last year were in your shoes (if you're heading for a one year degree, I'm not sure how they run it, but I'm sure they have an analogy – maybe it's run by career services). They'll start a rigorous curriculum of educating you about what consulting is and what case interviews are. Sounds great! That's all you need, right? In theory yes, the problem is, second years who got a summer internship still haven't been interviewer trained, and are frankly unsure about how or why they succeeded in their own interviews, so their advice is well meant, but not always applicable to you. They'll also turn out to be curiously unable to describe to you exactly what consulting is.

More Classes.

More clubs.

More study group. A lot more.

Week Four. Recruiting

Yes, you read that correctly. You've so far been here for three weeks of your two year sabbatical. You've had a total of three waking hours when you weren't working or partying, and you've had one hour with your career counselor, most of which was logistical stuff like how to use the website. Now recruiting has started, and these guys mean business.

Every day there will be top companies on campus. They'll buy you a sandwich, and you can sit and watch their presentation. They'll use a lot of PowerPoint. They'll have a lot of members of their team standing at the front of their room. After the PowerPoint overkill, you and more than a hundred of your classmates will follow the consultants to a reception room where they'll buy you a glass of wine and you'll realize you have to stand around in packs, trying to stand out, trying to think of an interesting question, with the goal that when the consultant returns to her hotel room or office that evening, she will remember you as the student who simply has to be interviewed.

Week Five. More recruiting events.

A lot more. Perhaps some intimate dinners (some of which you may be invited to, some of which you'll only hear about later) where students will have the chance to talk with senior partners about how fantastic and employable they (the students) are.

Final exams. Yes, that's right. This is a short term, kind of a boot-camp immersion experience to really get you in the mood. So five weeks after arriving, and four weeks after starting classes, you're taking final exams. And you like to do well in exams, so you've been studying all weekend, and now you're very stressed, because you haven't yet got a sense of whether you're any good at this new MBA stuff.

Visit to the medical center. Burning the candle at both ends like you have been doing is inevitably going to take its toll on your body. You're not invincible. You will get ill. Everybody does.

Week Six. Consulting trek

Finally you get a few days off between final exams and the start of next term. This is perhaps the time you thought you'd get to head back home, maybe go to a friend's wedding. Maybe you had your heart set on a few nights of proper sleep.

Unfortunately, you need to be in the city for these three days, for a marathon of office visits. Now it's getting serious. Now you're on their home turf, and you're wearing name tags that they've thoughtfully provided. And now you've already had one chance to network, so this time they're expecting your questions to be insightful, your personal connections to be meaningful. By the end of this trek, many firms will have decided for the most part on who they want to interview, and who they think they'll be making offers to.

Wait a minute! You haven't even had the chance to find out what being a consultant really means. You certainly haven't had time to find out what's the secret sauce that make a good consultant, and you absolutely have no idea how the companies are testing you for that sauce. But at the same time, you are in the middle of <u>the only chance you'll get in your life</u> to recruit with these guys – a chance that many people will never get, because these are some of the most selective and desired employers on the planet.

So... that's why I'm writing this book now, with the goal that you'll be reading it at your leisure, perhaps on the beach, perhaps on the plane. Because there really is quite a lot of information I've got for you. And some of it will require quiet contemplation and reflection. And you won't have a minute for it once you get here!

What is consulting?

In this chapter we'll find out that consulting companies are curiously unable to easily describe what they do.

We'll find out that even when they do succeed in getting across the 'what', they do not tell you 'how' they do it, so that it's very difficult to build up an understanding of what you'd do as a consultant.

We'll address this problem by going through some sample consulting experiences.

What do consultants do?

When I was at business school, this was the question I really wanted an answer to. Naturally I was reluctant to come straight out and ask the visiting recruiters, as I didn't want them to take me for some guy who couldn't even do the basic research himself.

Of course I went to the websites of the major companies. I asked classmates who had come from consulting. The problem was, nobody was able to give me a simple answer.

Part of the reason is that consulting is a very general term. What one management consultant does may vary widely from what another one does. But you'd think there are enough common features to be able to easily describe the basics of the job.

Another reason is that I think consulting is a very insular world. When you are doing it, it tends to become all consuming, and you forget that other people (your friends and family for instance) aren't going through what you are. So consultants, despite the fact that they're usually very clever, and are trained to be good communicators, have difficulty imagining just how little the outside world knows about their job.

What do consultants say about what they do?

If you attend a briefing by a consulting company (and if you are headed for business school you will hopefully get the opportunity to do this) here are some of the things you may well hear. Note that they don't give you a very clear understanding of what they do. They definitely don't give you any clue about what you might be doing as part of your average day as a consultant.

(I'm going to be flippant here about the kinds of things you'll hear. That's not because I want to suggest the companies don't do good work, but it is fair to say I think they're lacking in their ability to describe that work).

"We solve the most important problems for leaders of some of the World's biggest companies"

This is the kind of statement that may be technically correct, but is not exclusive to consultants. Therefore it's not very useful.

First of all, what are the most important problems a CEO has?

Some of them might be personal, for which you could apply the above statement to a psychologist, a surgeon, a marriage guidance counselor, a priest, a lawyer, and so on.

Let's assume we're looking at business problems. If I'm the CEO of an oil company, and my oil well is leaking oil into the ocean, the person solving my biggest problem may be a diver, or an engineer. If I'm the CEO of a mobile phone manufacturer, and I'm worried that nobody is buying my device, the person who solves my problem may be a product designer, or maybe an investment banker who manages to sell my company at a good price before it's too late, or maybe a film director who comes up with a genius commercial to sell my products.

So if we believe the above, a consultant may be a doctor, or a priest, or a film director, or a diver, or a product designer. This is a fairly broad category of jobs and I don't think we've gained any enlightenment on what a first year consultant at BCG does when he sits down at his desk.

"We work in teams"

Good for you.

"We bring analytical rigor to bear on our clients' problems"

What does that mean? Are we assuming that currently the director of sales at a company that is losing sales is not looking at his sales numbers? Are we perhaps to believe that the answers to our client's most pressing problems were there all along if only she had asked her CFO to 'run some numbers'?

I assume it means consultants don't do shoddy work, or jump to conclusions.

It's a bit like a car mechanic saying "I use accurate and functioning tools when I work on your car."

"We break down problems into their component parts and work in a team to solve them"

This one is interesting, because I can start to get my head around this. Breaking things down into their component parts sounds similar to what I might do when I paint my house, for instance. First I buy the paint, then I clear the room, then I strip the wallpaper etc. Perhaps this is what consultants do?

Or maybe it's like in one of those many forensics dramas on tv – one part of the team might run the fingerprints, while another looks at DNA?

Painting or crime scene investigation? Which one is it?

Again, this is telling me something about the way they work, but not what the work is.

"We work hard to ensure our solutions are implemented, not left sitting on a shelf"

From what I've heard from all the briefings, I have to infer that a while ago there was a consulting company that was famous for spending months at a client, billing large amounts of money, and putting together large reports. The client would then take these reports, thank the company, and put the reports on the shelf, where they would gather dust.

I believe this because at every single consulting company presentation I've ever been to, an earnest senior partner has announced that theirs is not like this. Their reports do not sit on the shelf.

Did that company ever exist? Perhaps. Presumably it didn't last very long because it wouldn't have got any repeat business. Would you hire a company again if the last time you had them in they sold you a million dollar bookend?

Again, this leaves me slightly unclear as to what the work is. I know a sports coach might work hard to ensure his advice is followed. I know a pharmacist, or a drug company, might like to believe that you take the pills for the full regime, rather than stopping as soon as you start to feel better. I can imagine that an architect gets a lot more job satisfaction when her design actually gets built, rather than gathering dust.

So which one of the above is a management consultant? Architect? Pharmacist? Sports Coach?

"We consistently add value to our clients"

Isn't that the central idea behind capitalism? You only hire people, or buy goods, if you believe you are getting some kind of value?

I think we can assume that if a company is succeeding in business to the point where it can afford to come to one of the world's top universities to hire some of the most expensive and sought after business graduates, then that company has come up with a formula whereby its services are seen as providing some kind of value.

My perspective on what consulting is

I'm going to approach this by attacking a number of questions:

- What do we mean when we say 'consulting'?
- Why might clients hire a consultant?
- What companies are out there and what trends has the industry seen in recent years?
- If I were a first year (post MBA) consultant, what would I be doing?
- How does the job evolve over time?
- What are the ups and downs of being a consultant?

First, let's try to define our terms here. In other words, what do we mean when we say consulting?

Here at business school we tend to use the label 'consulting', but actually that covers a lot of other businesses as well. For example, a consultant might also be an expert doctor.

I think we are talking about 'management consulting'.

Firms we are typically talking about include the 'big 3' global players (Bain, BCG, McKinsey), as well as other global players (including Deloitte, Accenture, A.T.Kearney etc.) and a lot of smaller firms (for the smaller ones I'm only really familiar with those that are based in the U.S. or Europe, and here we might be talking about companies like L.E.K., Mars & Co, Roland Berger, Altman Vilandrie and many, many more.)

Not just strategy

When students arrive here, many of them talk about 'strategy consulting'. I think this is because they have come from a similar firm which also described itself as a consultant, but did non-strategy work – often implementation of software for instance. They are anxious to clarify the difference in part because they want to move from their old firm to a new one.

It's not necessary to get hung up on whether the work is strategy or not. McKinsey's website, for instance, lists 8 functional practices. Strategy is one, alongside Operations, Business Technology, Corporate Finance, Marketing and Sales, Organization, Risk, and Sustainability. A consultant might join the firm aiming to do 'strategic' work, and end up choosing to become an expert in one of the other functional areas. Some other firms specialize in only one function.

Industry focus may or may not be included
It's also not necessary for now to clarify which industries our firms cover. Again, the big global companies will consult to most, if not all, industry groups. Other, small firms, may focus on fewer industries, or may specialize in only one industry.

Why might a client hire a consulting company?
This is a generalization, and so I am sure we can come up with examples that don't fit into the following categories, but by and large, a consultant is an external resource that is brought into a client for one or both of the following reasons:

- The client needs external advice/opinion
- The client needs temporary resource

These two things cover quite a lot, so let's look at some examples.

External advice

There are times when you don't have all the answers and you need to get another opinion or outside expertise
Even in a person's life, we could think of a range of situations, ranging from the trivial (do I look good in this shirt?), to the life or death (Doctor, what's this lump?).

At the start of this range, we have situations where outside counsel is not essential, but useful. Here we have situations where you could probably go and get the knowledge or expertise yourself, but it might take time.

At the other end, we have situations where knowledge is so specialized, and has often taken such a lot of time and resource to acquire, that we simply can't replicate it ourselves.

How might these situations play out in business?

Let's start with the 'not essential but useful' end of the spectrum (the business equivalent of asking for another point of view)
Imagine you own a chain of family restaurants. You feel that you haven't been making as much money as you think you should, and you're also aware that maybe consumer tastes have changed since you first came onto the scene.

As the owner, you probably have a good feeling for what's going on. You're an expert in this business after all, and you've got your finger on the pulse. You probably know other restaurant owners, and you keep abreast of trends in the business. In addition to all of your own resources, you have members of staff who you trust, and they also have informed opinions.

In many cases, you might rely on your own sense of what to do.

Sometimes, however, you might find it useful to have someone from outside the company also look at the situation and present you with an opinion.

How can someone from outside give you an opinion that's better than yours?

This is very similar to the question that my parents asked me when I told them I was going to be a consultant – how can you (with your lack of expertise in anything useful) advise leaders who have decades of experience?

It's true. The disadvantage of getting an outsider is that they're not going to know the business as well as you, but remember you're only asking their opinion; you're not handing over the reins.

There are a number of advantages of getting outside advice:

Firstly, an outsider won't start their research with any preconceptions about your business. Perhaps you and everyone who works for you take it for granted that people like antlers on the walls of family restaurants – it's worked for years, you just don't question it. But an outsider, maybe even an outsider who hasn't worked before in family restaurants, will be able to have a fresh perspective. Sometimes even just having someone ask the question – 'hey, why are there antlers all over the place', can set you thinking and lead to a useful discovery.

As the outsider won't start with the benefit of knowing what 'everybody knows', they'll often have to base their research on a lot more data and facts than your own staff would use. Your staff may have a feeling that profits have been declining, but an outsider might start by getting all the sales figures for the last ten years, and really digging into these, to see if that feeling is correct, and to see if there is anything else going on. This is what leads to the talk about 'fact-based' and 'rigorous analysis'.

Secondly, an outsider doesn't have to stick around, so they're not so bound by the rules of internal politics. It may be that everybody in your company knows that the real reason for declining profits is that the chef's recipes aren't really all that good, but maybe the chef is a really great guy and nobody wants to hurt his feelings. Even more difficult – what if the problem is actually you? Which of your staff is going to tell you that?

Thirdly, an outsider may not know your business inside out, but what if you hire someone who's spent the last five years working for different types of restaurants around the world? They'd probably be able to bring some new ideas simply from what they've seen work, and not work, elsewhere. Even if they haven't worked in restaurants, having someone come along who's worked in different industries may provide some interesting counterpoints. Perhaps your consultant previously worked for an airline that was also experiencing declining revenues. Perhaps there are some parallels between airlines and restaurants that they can bring to bear.

Let's look at a different (slightly negative, but entirely believable) situation.
Let's say you are the Chief Executive of a global retailer. Your share price has been sliding and the brand of your stores has been eroding.

You have a responsibility to your shareholders, represented by the Board of Directors, to maximize the value of the investment they've made.

There's a company of consultants that is known as the world's expert in global retail. They are expensive, but their fees are a drop in the ocean compared to your currently sliding share price and brand value.

Let's say you don't hire this company. You're the expert after all – you were on the front cover of Business Week when you were hired a few years ago.

Now let's fast forward to one year later, and the decline has continued. You're called before the Board, and as they tell you that you're no longer the Chief Executive, they ask "Why didn't you hire company X to advise you?" Now you look back at the half a million dollars a team from company X would have cost, and you realize it would have been a pretty good investment – hopefully they would have helped you turn the company around, but even if not, at least you'd have shown that you did everything a responsible CEO should do.

Next time (hopefully you get a next time) you are in charge, you'll probably go and hire company X as a matter of course, so that if things go wrong, you can say "Hey, I hired company X, and I've followed their advice." As I said, this has a somewhat negative connotation of using consultants as 'insurance', but it's human nature to want some kind of insurance.

Another situation around insurance...
Let's say you're a middle manager at a massive company. You've got an idea for how to improve things, but your company is very slow to listen, and even slower to act. You do, however, have a budget for consultants, because the company believes that consultants bring value.

You call up your friend at consulting company Z – maybe someone you went to business school with, back in the good old days. You hire company Z and ask them to do some work to validate your good idea. They do the work, come up with a lot more evidence than you'd have been able to gather, and accompany you to the meeting with the board, where you and your buddy from business school present a watertight argument for why your idea is the next big thing.

In this case, it wasn't you who wanted the insurance of expert opinion, it was the board.

We could view this in a negative light, and say "why didn't the senior leaders trust their guy when he had the good idea", or we could take a positive view and say "here's a guy who's going places – he had a great idea, he hired the right consultants to help him flesh it out, and now he's making it happen." I don't have a strong opinion about the 'right or wrong' of this, but I do know that this scenario sounds very believable and if I were the buddy from business school who was now a partner at consulting company Z I'd feel good about the fact that I'd helped develop the evidence for why this idea was great, I'd played a part in helping a big company improve the way it works, and most importantly that I'd helped a friend advance his career.

Now let's look at the other end of the 'advice' spectrum – when you really need an expert.
Let's go back to the family restaurant business. Things are going well, and over the last few years you've expanded from 5 to 50 restaurants all

over the state. You're at a conference and you hear about a colleague who took his business from 50 restaurants to 5,000 across the globe, and just sold his share of the business to a private equity group for more money than you'd need to retire happily ever after.

As you go back to your hotel room that night, you're probably asking yourself – how the heck do I do that?

Now you're in a situation where you are really out of your comfort zone. You started out as a burger chef twenty years ago. Then you were a competent manager of several local restaurants, and now you own 50 restaurants. You're a restaurant guy, not a global businessman, and you certainly don't know how you could get on track to having thousands of restaurants.

Let's say you heard of a consulting company that specialized in advising people like you – they have a whole roster of clients who have all gone from a handful of properties to global players. Wouldn't you be interested in talking with a partner at that company, and hearing about how they could help you be the next Ronald MacDonald?

This is a bit like one of those times in your personal life when you really can't do it yourself. It's like selling your house – you really need a lawyer who does this all the time.

Sometimes there are even laws or regulations that require you to get an expert
If I want to install a new gas appliance in my house, my local building codes say I can't do it myself – I need to get someone who is licensed to do this work – he has received up to date training and is sure to know how to do this work safely.

Similarly, let's say I was the European head of manufacturing for a global car manufacturer. My boss, the Chief Executive, has announced that we are going to move much of our manufacturing to China – to be closer to the fastest growing customer base. Let's say my European staff, some of whom I need to make redundant, and some of whom I want to keep, are members of a union, and let's say I've previously signed agreements with that union that I won't make any redundancies without proper investigation and consultation.

It may well be the case that I am obliged to show that I have done my research to show that moving the manufacturing jobs is best for the company. For this I'll need an independent, outside expert, a company that is respected not just by my management but also by the unions. If I mess this up, all of my staff in Europe may go on strike, and global manufacturing may grind to a halt. I'm certainly going to hire that outside expert.

External Resource

There are times when everybody in your company is busy, and you don't want to hire more full time staff, but there are important things that need to get done.
This is quite easy to get your head around. Sometimes you just need some temporary resource. If it's a job that is fairly easy, or is one that many people are skilled at, there'll be agencies that can provide the staff and you won't need consultants. So where do consultants fit into this picture?

Firstly, the job might be at the level of someone in your organization who is fairly senior, or requires a high level of functional or industry expertise, and there simply aren't temp agencies who specialize in this kind of thing. You could go through a recruiting process and hire somebody on a part time basis, but for a very important piece of work, you'd want to put a lot of time and effort into that process to make sure you got a high quality candidate.

What's great about a consulting company in this instance is that they act as aggregators of clever, hard-working people. For instance, they've already done the job of scouring the world's top universities, where they only hired the top students, so you can be sure that if you call them and ask them to send a team, or perhaps just one consultant, you're not going to be getting a dud.

Let's look at an example.

You're the South America Head of customer satisfaction at a global engineering company. You get an email from head office asking for a detailed report on ways your division could simultaneously cut costs and increase customer satisfaction. The deadline is one month away. You don't have time to do this, and your teams are all busy. What do you do?

This is a one-off request for work that requires resource beyond what you have. It doesn't make sense to hire someone, and even if you could, it would take longer than a month to find that person and get them started.

In this case, it's fairly easy to imagine that you'd pick up the phone to a consulting company, give them the specs of what you require, negotiate a price, and then expect to have a team on the ground the next day. They can devote the whole of the next month to doing all the work on the report, you will check in frequently and ensure it has your 'voice', and that you understand everything in it, so that when you fly to head office and present it, you'll be seen as the author. Or, if yours is a company that values consultants, you may even publicize the fact that you got company X to do the work – perhaps it will add gravitas to the findings.

If you think about it, outsourcing work like this can actually be very efficient. When you have the demand, you get hard working people on the ground the next day. When you don't have the demand, they're gone.

Many companies and organizations deliberately resource themselves in a lean way, knowing that when the busy times come along, they can get consultants in.

Consultants as turbo boost

Another element of the above story that consultants bring is the ability to inject a different level of pace. If you hire someone onto your team, they'll adopt the culture of your company, go home at the same time as everyone else, and so on. If time is of the essence, you can essentially pay a consulting team to act as a 'turbo-boost'. Of course you'll pay for it, but you'll get results very quickly, and perhaps you'll help create a sense of urgency throughout the organization.

This is actually one of the areas where consultants can be most effective. It is also one of the areas that can create the most friction. In most organizations, people have a lot of work on their plates, and they divide up their time over the coming weeks so that they can make gradual progress on everything they are working on. Let's say I'm a junior consultant, and you work in accounts at Big Cereal Co. My consulting company has been retained to produce a report proving the Finance Director's feeling that many divisions are spending too much on expenses. It's my job to get all expense claims for the past 5 years. You hold this information, but it's not all in one place, and to get it all will involve about a day's work. But your plate is already full for the next week. So when I email you, asking for the data, you'll look at that email and mentally assign it to next Monday. That's a problem for me, because my manager is going to ask me in two hours' time where that data is. That now becomes a problem for you because I'll be on the phone to you asking for the data now. If you don't give it to me, I'll come and sit on the edge of your desk, asking for the data. You can see that this has the potential to not end happily for anyone involved.

What companies are out there?

There are a great many companies out there, and sometimes just understanding the landscape can be quite daunting. If your sole goal is to work as a management consultant it can sometimes be helpful to think of a number of dimensions by which you can filter the whole set. For instance, if you know you want to live and work in a particular city, then that is a useful starting point. If you have experience in, or passion for, a particular industry, that can also be a good starting point. If you are networking, then sometimes the filter is literally just 'who can I find and where do they work?' There's nothing wrong with being opportunistic in that way, as long as it gets you started.

One more thought – many people I work with tend to think this is a one-shot deal. If they don't get their dream company now, they will move on to another type of company and give up on the consulting goal. This isn't at all necessary. For many people, a career will encompass many moves, so if you want to end up with a dream company like Bain or McKinsey, for instance, it may well make sense to start out somewhere else and build your consulting credentials. This is particularly true if you are early on in your career, or just graduating from university. Getting into the industry and putting in some solid years at a respectable company is a good stepping stone between where you are now and where you want to end up.

So who is out there?

Global, premium brand (MBB, also known in consulting as the big 3)

If you type 'most prestigious consulting companies' into a search engine, these three will always come up – McKinsey & Company, Bain & Company and The Boston Consulting Group (BCG), which we'll refer to as McKinsey, Bain and BCG.

These three companies are so desirable they've earnt their own acronym amongst the community of aspiring consultants – MBB. McKinsey, Bain and BCG are seen by many as the ultimate in terms of brand recognition and quality. But what do people mean by that, and why is it important?

The main selling point of these firms is that they hire the best people. This sounds elitist, and to a certain extent it is. What they mean by the best people is that they hire people who in their opinion are most intelligent, most hard-working, and best at people skills. What this means to a client is that they are going to get some of the most clever and hard working people around working on their problem – and that includes everyone from partner down to analyst.

An interesting outcome of this for the firm, is that in economic terms, they can probably have their 'resources' (consultants) turning out work that is a higher quality, and at a higher volume than their competitors, so they can do the work more quickly or simply promise a higher quality end product. For both of these things they can charge a premium.

For the consultants who work at these firms, the brand advantage comes into play most strongly when they are looking to move on in their career. There are whole headhunting companies out there that specialize in recruiting alumni from the big 3 consulting firms. It is not uncommon to see a job spec from a potential recruiter that specifies as one of the requirements – x years experience at a top tier strategy firm.

The other principal advantage for consultants is the alumni network. Each of the top tier firms invest significant resources in cultivating their alumni network – holding events, making connectivity easy, and for each of the firms it is a true asset to be able to reach out to someone you've never met before, identify yourself as a fellow alum, and have that as a starting point. When you do that, both of you enter the conversation knowing a lot about the training each has received, the experiences and ways of working you have been through, and the 'quality' of the person in terms of intellect, work ethic and so on. You can see why this is a powerful tool in a consultant's onward career.

Global, accounting companies (Big 4)

The other major category in terms of large consulting companies is Big 4 accounting companies that have consulting arms – Deloitte, EY, PWC and KPMG. Of these, Deloitte's consulting arm is the largest, although the other companies have recently been expanding rapidly via acquisition (about which we'll talk more later). The principal advantage these firms have is that their accounting and financial service parent companies have existing relationships with many, if not all, of the world's major companies, so they are able to win consulting work as a result. In addition, when serving a consulting client, these companies can offer a great many other specialties should the need arise.

Global, technology focused

There are a number of very large consulting companies that are known to focus less on strategy work, and more on technology. Among these are Accenture, IBM, Capgemini and Tata Consulting. Working at one of these companies is likely to involve longer projects with more of an implementation and tech focus.

Mid-sized generalist firms

As we move down the scale in terms of size of firm, we reach a segment that has been going through a lot of change. Only a few years ago there were a number of firms in this segment, including Monitor, Booz, and The Parthenon Group. These have all recently been acquired by the Big 4 accounting firms. A number of firms still 'survive' independently in this group, including L.E.K., Simon Kucher, Mercer and Roland Berger. If we think of the large global firms serving most industries in most geographies, in this segment we see companies serving a subset – often with an industry focus, and often with a geographic focus. The work may well be very similar, and indeed many of these firms will routinely compete with the larger firms, but the range of work open to a consultant may be less varied.

Boutique consulting firms

Boutique consulting firms offer specialized advice, and this specialization is usually by industry. For instance, there are many firms out there that specialize in healthcare, and within healthcare there are many that specialize in a certain facet, such as how a pharma company should price a new drug, or how a hospital could run more efficiently. The work done at such companies may be similar to that at a large company, but as with the mid-sized generalists, there will be less choice and diversity for its consultants. On the flipside, consultants at a boutique are more likely to quickly develop their own expertise.

Internal consulting groups

To add to the mix, many large companies have internal consulting groups, and these groups often do very similar work to the management consultants we have started to talk about. Very often these internal groups compete with external consultants for work, and may be staffed with people who started out in external consulting companies. When these internal groups do work that is largely the same as external firms, we'll also consider them included under our 'consulting' umbrella.

So what does this mean for someone looking to work in consulting?

This rather bewildering array of types of companies can sometimes overwhelming. If your goal is simply to work in consulting, then you should probably consider a bit further what exactly it is you are looking for.

Here are some reasons that many of the people I work with end up focusing on a particular sector. Perhaps some of these reasons will resonate with you.

MBB

- You want a stamp of approval on your resume that shows you were good enough to get hired by one of the most selective companies in the world.

- You want a broad range of onward opportunities because you don't yet know which industry or type of work you want to specialize in, whether you stay in consulting or if you leave.
- You want to work with some of the smartest and most hard working people in the world, in a setting that will continually challenge you.
- You want to be exposed to some of the most difficult, high level problems faced by the most senior leaders of the world's largest and most important companies and organizations.
- You want a lifetime membership in an elite alumni network.

Big 4 accounting
- You want to work in an organization where there are colleagues from other aspects of financial service and advisory
- You want a consulting company that is backed by the resources of a significantly larger parent company
- You want a diverse consulting experience.

Global, technology focused
- You have a particular interest in, and experience in technology.
- You want to see a project through at one company that may take multiple years, probably working at a pace that is more akin to regular office life

Mid-sized generalist
- You have some sense of which industry or geography you want to focus on.
- You want a firm where it still may be small enough that many of the partners know each other, and you will not just be a number.

Boutique
- You already have expertise in a certain field, or you are sure you want to develop it
- You want a firm where there are a relatively small number of employees

Internal

- You want to be a consultant but you also want to work for one company, so that you can build up an expertise, and perhaps a future career path.
- You want to spend more of your time doing the work, and less time pitching for work
- You want a more manageable lifestyle (often internal consultants work at a more regular pace than their external counterparts)

Big vs small

One key dimension amongst the above categories is big vs small. It's worth thinking about the difference between a company of 10,000 employees and one with 20.

The large company will certainly have a lot more resources, and this will show in a number of ways. When you want a new computer, they will have people who will get it for you. Likewise a flight or a hotel. When you need training, you will probably be trained with a cohort of people from your own company. On the downside, you will never know everyone in your company, and even in your office. You may have to get very good at internal networking just to get staffed. You will certainly have to modify the way you work to fit in with the way that the rest of the 9,999 people work.

With a small company, there will be times when you will be frustrated by the lack of back office support. You may even need to book your own flights or source your own equipment. You may get training materials from a third party, or attend training with people from other companies. On the other hand, you'll probably get to know all of your colleagues really well, and will benefit from working in a place where people know you. There may be more leeway for you to work in a way that suits you, not the system.

These are all generalizations, by necessity, but you can start to see that there are definitely differences between, let's say, a twenty person pharma pricing company and a 50,000 person tech consulting firm. Many of these differences will materially affect your everyday working experience, your likelihood of getting the job in the first place, and your onward career options.

What recent trends have shaped the consulting landscape?

In recent years, the world of management consulting has seen a number of interesting trends, even since the time when I was recruiting at business school (ten years ago).

The major trends have been:

- Consolidation
- Increasing focus on implementation

Consolidation

As discussed above, a significant number of small and mid-sized consulting companies have been acquired in recent years. What does this mean for the prospective consultant?

Firstly, there are fewer companies for you to apply to. This matters to the extent that more companies in the same space gave more chances to get it right in the interview, so now if you are interviewing with less companies you have to be extra sure to get it right first time.

On the upside, the companies that have been acquired have now been given mandates to grow, and the resources to do so. The chances of getting hired by the firms formerly known as Parthenon, Monitor, Axia and Booz are probably better than ever, now that they have deep pocketed parent companies wanting to maximize the value of their acquisitions.

Probably the main thing on the lips and minds of people in the industry as a result of this consolidation is the discussion of whether this means that there is no longer room for the small to mid-sized consulting company. Are they in some way now unable to compete? The main argument is that without a certain scale they are unable to serve large clients on the full range of issues. This is closely tied in with the next point – that even the larger and more prestigious firms are moving more and more to offer a diverse array of service that is increasingly far away from the traditional three month strategy project.

For an aspiring consultant, the ramifications are that if you choose to join one of the remaining mid-sized companies, presumably there is the chance that your company will at some point in the future go through an acquisition. In my experience from talking to consultants working at acquired firms, there have not been layoffs, apart from perhaps in the back office. Think about it – when a large company acquires a smaller consulting firm, they are deliberately acquiring the people in that firm, so it is unlikely that they will make cuts. In fact, they will probably ramp up hiring significantly to make more of the brand of the company they have acquired. Probably the biggest day to day change after the acquisition will be a change in culture, as you experience the change from being part of a small, independent organization, to being part of a larger company.

Probably the most likely outcome of this wave of consolidation is that the remaining small to medium sized firms will have to become known as specialists in some field, becoming to a certain extent large boutiques. A mid-sized company with a strong position in a field, such as healthcare, or marketing for instance, will presumably still be able to bring a solid mix of expertise plus scale.

Another thing to bear in mind is if you are joining a small firm that has aspirations of becoming a mid-sized firm – is this expansion plan realistic, and if so, what is it about the firm that will give it a sustainable position in this position?

Increasing focus on implementation

When I was at business school ten years ago, each major consulting company had one available job I could apply for – consultant. Now, in addition to that role, such companies are hiring a large number of other positions, all under the broad banner of 'consulting'. These are some of the consulting roles that major consulting companies have posted in the last year.

- Sales implementation consultant
- Senior implementation consultant
- Senior implementation coach
- Organization solutions coach
- Oil & gas implementation consultant
- Healthcare implementation coach
- Corp. and business functions implementation coach
- Metals and mining implementation coach
- Strategic sourcing and procurement consultant
- Supply chain consultant
- Federal functional consultant
- Big data consultant
- Financial project management office analyst

One of the words you'll notice pops up a lot in the above list is 'implementation'. So what's that all about?

In the not-too distant past, the majority of consulting work at a major firm was short term in nature and advisory. The average length of project was 6 weeks to 3 months, and would result in an 'answer' – often in the form of a presentation or report.

What happened to that answer? Usually one of three things:

1. It was received gratefully but ultimately ignored because the readers of the report didn't truly believe the answer.

2. A different (probably cheaper) outside consulting company was brought in to help implement the answer, in a long-term project that probably spanned a number of years.
3. An internal team was used to help implement the answer, which was a challenge because the internal team was not expert at such work.

You can see why there has been a shift towards implementation:

1. If the client doesn't implement the answer you gave them, then they won't get the value from it. Much better if you can come up with a way that increases the likelihood of them implementing. Part of this is about getting the client more involved in the creation of the answer, but a large part is about getting more involved in the implementation itself.
2. If someone is going to get paid to do the implementation – let's try to make sure that it's us! There's a lot of money in implementation, and if it requires a different skills set then let's invest in that.
3. If internal resources will be used, how about if we support them? Again, we may need to change our working model to work more at their pace, and in a way that suits them, but that would be worthwhile.

So you can see the logic above, and the result is that many if not all of the major consulting companies are moving into implementation.

What this means for someone seeking to work in consulting is that there are now more opportunities, particularly for people with some degree of industry experience. Implementation means getting things done, which requires skills both in terms of how a particular business works, and also in terms of how to get people to change their behavior. Some of these skills can be learnt by a relative newcomer, but largely they rely on experience. This is good news for people currently working in the relevant industry, especially with experience of making things happen.

What does a first year consultant actually do?

This is the big question. It's the one that everyone in the consulting club wants answered, and is often expressed as 'describe a typical day', or 'what do you do when you turn up at the office?'

I'm going to make some assertions here that are mostly true. If you set out with the goal of disproving me, you'll find it very easy to find examples of activities that I don't cover. I'm not going for exhaustive, absolute truth here, I'm trying to give you a general idea.

First, let's run through a couple of 'day in the life' examples:

Scenario 1:

You are a recent MBA graduate. You graduated in June, and spent the summer taking a well-deserved break and then moving to Chicago, where you will be working for ABC consulting. You started work in September, and your first two weeks were taken up by training. Part of this was a global training program, where you joined all the recent MBA grads at a resort in Colorado.

Training

We gave you your computer, and gave you some catch-up classes on PowerPoint and Excel. We presume that you all used these a lot at business school, but different schools have different ways of learning, so we give you some basic lessons just in case.

We ran some day-long role-plays of client interaction. Here we were careful to give you the benefit of our thinking on how to work with challenging clients, because our biggest fear is that as a new consultant you will embarrass ABC consulting and cause us to lose a client.

We threw a huge amount of money at you via the medium of alcohol, partly because we want you to know that we're very generous and successful, and partly because we want your new cohort to bond, thus providing you with a support network of friends who are going through the same experience at the same time.

While you were being trained, you also caught up on some of the unofficial knowledge circulating in the company. You found out what you should pack in your carry-on bag, you learnt who are the managers and partners that nobody wants to work with, you heard some stories of some people who started three years ago and who are now almost partners, and you also heard plenty more stories of people who started within the last three years and have now left.

First project

Your first project was in an industry that you have some familiarity with, and the main thing you noticed from the experience was that you were given feedback approximately a thousand times a day. You also noticed that invariably that feedback was negative, and that apparently ABC consulting has some very fixed ways of doing things that are not at all intuitive.

Now:

It's day one of your second project. I'm your manager. You woke up at 4am, and at 4.30 a luxury car was idling outside your apartment building, waiting to take you to the airport. This is your first travel project, so you spent most of last night repacking your travel case. Inside the case you have three clean shirts, three sets of underwear, toiletries that will be allowed through airport security, your iPad, your gym clothes and sneakers.

As you sit in the car, you notice that the light is blinking on your device – apparently you got some mail since you last checked it at 11pm last night. You have an email from the partner on the project you're just starting – welcoming you to the team and offering his time in case you have any questions about the industry or the client. You also have an email from the travel department, letting you know that you are booked into the same hotel as your manager, not the one you asked for. There's an email from one of your new friends from training in Colorado, she is also starting a new project today, although it seems that somehow hers started yesterday, because she is already asking all of your cohort if anyone happens to have a model that can predict the shopping patterns of customers in malls in Dubai.

At the airport you head to the lounge, where you notice a lot of people dressed very similarly to you (you're wearing a suit, as ABC consulting is fairly formal). You notice that they all have their laptops open and they all appear to be working. As you sip your coffee you open your own laptop, and flick through some PowerPoint slides that I sent you last week. These give you an overview of the client, showing some of the previous work we've done there.

You board the plane, and again you notice that all the other consultants have their laptops open, so you open yours and pretend to work.

You land in Memphis, pick up a hire car, and drive out to the client site. As you stand at the reception desk, waiting while they print you an ID tag, you call me and I come down to meet you.

We walk up to the team room (a small room in their building that the client has lent to us for the duration of the project), and there you find five other consultants from ABC consulting, all focusing on their laptops. I introduce you, and you find that there are actually two teams here – ours, and another team that is working on an IT project.

You and I head to the coffee concession inside the client building and we talk about the project. I ask you what you are hoping to learn from this project, what feedback you got from your last project, and how you are feeling about living Monday thru Thursday in a hotel for the next 3 months.

I tell you that your part of this project is going to be an analysis of the way our client encourages innovation amongst its staff. After a while of me talking you realize you should be taking notes, so you get out your notepad (you've noticed everyone at ABC consulting carries a notepad) and start writing.

Your job is going to involve a number of pieces. Firstly, I want you to talk with the HR department and find out how the firm currently thinks about innovation. Then I want you to gather as much information as you can about rivals of our client, to show how they do it. I also want you to set up calls with experts within our consulting company – you'll have to find out who has this expertise – and put together some kind of primer on 'best practices'. Finally I want you to bring all this together with a recommendation that clearly shows what our client should do to encourage more innovation.

I suggest we check in again at 4 this afternoon, and then perhaps you could show me an unpopulated 'ghost' PowerPoint document first thing tomorrow morning.

I also tell you that we have a call with the partner at 5 this afternoon, and ask you if you can book us a room where we can talk loudly into a speakerphone without any clients overhearing us. Also, be prepared to give an overview of your innovation work at this call – the partner loves innovation and is really excited to see what you're going to come up with.

In addition, I suggest that as you are the newest member of the team, you might like to arrange a team dinner for us tonight – somewhere fun. I ask you to get some options together and we can discuss them at 4.

Finally, I tell you that I've got a lot more material about the industry that I was meaning to send you last week – I'll email that to you now so that you can catch up on it.

At this point, your mind is buzzing with all of the things that you have to go and do before we next meet at 4pm (it's now 1pm). So you excuse yourself and head back to the team room.

First up, you call the client's reception desk and find out how you can book a meeting room with a speaker phone. The receptionist is able to help you, but you have no idea where the room she gives you is actually located, so you run down to reception to pick up a map. Then you decide to check out the route to the room, just in case. You find the room, poke your head in, notice that there is a speakerphone, and head back to the team room.

Next, you ask me who to speak with in HR about current innovation practices. I tell you I'll walk you over to HR in a few minutes and introduce you personally.

In the meantime, you send an email to your cohort from training asking if anyone has done anything on innovation. In a few minutes you get a PowerPoint deck from one of your friends. It contains some useful pages on ways to set up innovation units within companies. You call your friend, and it sounds like he is working on a very similar project (so to a certain extent he will be limited by your firm's rules about keeping client information confidential), and he gives you the names of some partners in ABC consulting who you should talk to.

You send emails to the assistants of the partners, and ask for time to get their thoughts on innovation.

You also do an online search for innovation, and start to gather available information on your client's competitors, although this is difficult.

Then I walk with you over to the HR department where I introduce you to our contact over there – she is someone who I know, and have worked with before, and she will help us get the information about what is currently going on at the client. In fact, it turns out that she has been working on a proposal for new ways to do innovation at the client for a while now, and is eager to discuss. You agree to meet with her tomorrow morning. You are pleased because she seems nice, perhaps this can be a person at the client that you can build a good relationship with.

Back at the team room, you ask for recommendations for restaurants. The team throw about twenty names at you, and you spend the next ten minutes online checking them all out.

At 4, you and I meet again, and you tell me about your progress. You remind me that I haven't yet sent the extra files about the client, and I say I'll do it later – you can read them this evening. I give you my thoughts on the restaurants, and you agree to make the reservation. You ask me what time to make the reservation for (this is a big moment), and I tell you that in the past few weeks we have been finishing up at the client by around 7, then heading back to the hotel, before heading out to eat at around 8. You breathe a sigh of relief. This is a lot better than some of the horror stories you heard at training.

After our catch-up, we head straight over to the conference room, where we have a call with the partner. You notice that I'm a little stressed about this.

It turns out the speaker phone in the conference room isn't plugged in, so we do the call on my phone – set on speaker mode. The partner is walking through an airport, and there is a lot of background noise, so we can hardly hear her. She starts by welcoming you to the team, and asking what you think of the client so far. You manage to say something about the nice person in HR you've met, and then I steer the conversation towards a review of our current work, and our plans for the rest of the week. I have a PowerPoint pack in front of me, and the partner frequently refers to a specific page, so she must have a copy in front of her too. The call seems fairly chaotic, but the partner does ask some salient questions which cause me to admit that there are some holes in our plan at present, and we subsequently pick up a few more things to put onto our 'to-do' list. The partner asks how your research is going on innovation, and gives you the names of some of her colleagues.

After the call, we huddle in the team room and discuss the ramifications of the new pieces of work the partner has suggested we do. The way we structure this conversation is largely around the PowerPoint pack. I lay the current pack out on the desk, and we talk about some new pages that might come out of the partner conversation. I also make some changes to some of the existing pages, and hand these edited pages to your colleague.

Luckily, your work doesn't seem to be affected.

While we wait for the taxi to arrive at 7, you get out some blank paper and draw out some rough sketches of some PowerPoint pages. You start with the story you will aim to tell, which goes something like "this is what you do in innovation…, this is what your competitors do…, this is what best practice looks like… this is therefore what you should plan to do… these are the steps you should take…" You then try to sketch out what kind of visual representation you might use to help get the message across. You decide you'll turn these drafts into actual PowerPoint pages later tonight, so that by tomorrow morning you can show me that you've made some real progress.

At 7, the taxi arrives, and we close up our laptops, grab our wheelie bags, and head out to the front door. You notice that all of the clients are long gone, and the building is dark. The other team that is sharing our team room remain at their desks, and appears to have no plans to leave anytime soon.

Scenario 2:

This is an article I wrote when I was a consultant at McKinsey. It was published at Tuck for students to read, and it has subsequently been posted online in a number of places.

6:35 a.m. I'm in the shower and the bathroom door opens. My two kids are up and want to say hi. I try to listen to my eldest daughter's monologue about the relative merits of Polly Pocket vs. Barbie but I'm not sure I catch every nuance. After a while I tell them to go back to bed, and that I'll come and wake them up once I'm out of the shower and dressed.

7:00 a.m. Finally dressed and ready for the day, I go and get the girls and they come downstairs with me, giving my wife an extra few minutes of sleep before she has to get up and start getting the girls ready for school. Since I don't often get home before the girls get to bed (7 p.m.) this is my main opportunity to see them during the week. Often I stay home longer and have breakfast with them, before heading off towards the office at about 8:15, but today I've got a breakfast meeting in town, so I talk to them while I put on my shoes and check my phone for emails. A few rounds of goodbye kisses and I'm out the door at 7:10.

7:10 a.m. I have a short drive to the station car park. We live in a small village outside London. It looks like it's going to be a nice day (not always guaranteed in summer in the U.K.!)—the sky is blue, the trees are green, I'm beginning to wake up, and life is good!

7:25 a.m. Strange how the train at this time is never particularly busy. If this was forty five minutes later I wouldn't get a seat, but now I manage to find a space next to the window and all of a sudden I have 22 minutes of undisturbed 'me time'. Often I use this time to get in a little more sleep, but today I'm in the middle of an intriguing book, The End of Mr. Y, which I eagerly dive into.

7:47 a.m. Walking through the newly refurbished St. Pancras International station is always uplifting. It was opened earlier in the year and is now London's terminal for the Eurostar. It's one of the most, if not the most beautiful public spaces I've ever seen — an immense Victorian gothic station with a glass roof, now filled with upscale bars and restaurants like the food court of an expensive mall. I get a particular childish thrill about walking past the Eurostar departure board which is listing the next train with its destination of Disneyland Paris. Not for me today though, I'm off to the tube station.

7:50 a.m. It's incredible how so many people can fit onto such a small underground train. Everyone is incredibly polite, ignoring the fact that we are pressed up against each other in a way that doesn't ordinarily happen without alcohol.

8:00 a.m. I'm having breakfast with my "Summer Buddy". He is a Summer Associate (our term for summer intern) and I have been assigned to him as someone to talk to during his time here. Since I was a 'summmer' two years ago I have a fairly good idea of what he is going through, and so am able to help steer him through some of the challenges of being dropped into McKinsey after a year of business school. After a week or so of trying to get together for dinner, we have decided that breakfast is a better bet as it is less likely to get cancelled by last minute team or project demands. Also, this means I have an excuse to come to the restaurant at Fortnum and Mason for breakfast. I like this restaurant primarily because it's the only place in England I've found so far that can make pancakes well, thus satisfying my craving for a reminder of my time at business school in America. My 'Summer Buddy' talks to me about his experience so far. He is keen to find out from me whether his team and his project are 'typical'—i.e., is he getting a good sample of life as a McKinsey consultant that will enable him to make an informed choice about whether to return next year. We talk about the fact that while there are many 'typical' ways of working, there are also many nuances that are unique to each team and project. In many ways I think this is why I like consulting (at least what I've seen of it in my 15 months so far)—there is a definite underlying skill set to build and rely on, but then each project and each team has its own quirks which keep me on my toes.

8:50 a.m. Breakfast over, I have a ten minute taxi journey to the client office. The route takes me past Buckingham Palace, where tourists are already gathering to take photos of their "holidays of a lifetime".

9:00 a.m. My current project ('study' in McKinsey parlance) is Top-Team Effectiveness for a large organization (at McKinsey we don't disclose the identities of our clients). Our usual working practice is to spend Monday thru Thursday at the client which ensures we bring the client along as we develop the solution, then Friday at our office to ensure we also have an opportunity to connect with each other, attend training, etc. Since my current client is ten minutes from our office, we are a lot more flexible, and often my day can involve several trips back and forth, depending on what we are doing and who we are meeting. We start today with a 'team huddle'—the three of us who form the core McKinsey team [Engagement Manager, Associate (me) and Business Analyst] get together over a coffee for ten minutes to discuss the day ahead. We each define what success will look like by the end of the day, and talk about some of the challenges we foresee.

9:30 a.m. Our study is focusing on the ways that the top leaders of this organization work together, and how this has an effect on the functioning of the entire organization. It has been a fascinating opportunity to work closely with the Chief Executive and her top team, particularly as we have been working with very sensitive areas like the way the staff perceive their leadership. Last week we hosted a day-long workshop for the top team in which we presented information we'd collected from the rest of the organization. Some of this was very challenging, and the day was very powerful, with a lot of soul-searching. It ended with some very clear resolutions that will mean large changes for the way the organization works. My task right now is to draft a memo from the Chief Executive to the staff, to let them know what was decided at the workshop and what will be the next steps.

10:00 a.m. When I've finished my first draft, I send it on to the Engagement Manager, who makes some edits and then sends it out to the partners who are overseeing our study. They will all send their comments back to me, and I'll assemble them into a final draft.

10:20 a.m. A lot of my time is spent checking and sending emails. Most are related to the current study, but a couple are worth mentioning to give an idea of the other 'ongoing issues' I am thinking about.

1. In the office, we have been running a 'summer exhibition' of artwork created by consultants and support staff. Our work has been displayed in the restaurant, and I entered two photos. Those of us who entered photos have been emailing each other about setting up a photo club, and we are going to meet tomorrow to discuss the next steps.

2. Next week I am off to Austria for two weeks' training. This is a course that consultants are sent on after approximately one year of experience.

3. Each year the London office chooses an 'office challenge'—something that everyone can get involved in. This year we are making a feature film about charities, and bearing in mind film production was my former profession I am arranging a meeting with some of the film-makers to offer advice.

11:10 a.m. I'm having a meeting with the client's Director of Communications, to discuss the draft letter from the Chief Executive. Over the past few weeks we have built up a good relationship, and the meeting is fairly relaxed and enjoyable. He has some concerns, though, about the correct way to get the information contained in the letter out to the staff, and we debate the relative merits of a memo from the Chief Executive versus a 'cascade' of more personal communications from each director to their direct reports, and so on down through the organization.

12:30 p.m. I am having a 'problem-solving' session with the Business Analyst (At McKinsey, BA's are younger team members hired from bachelor's degree level) on our team. Problem Solving is the term we use to cover a number of ways of team working, not unlike the way we work in study groups at business school. One of the outcomes of last week's workshop was that a key area of the business needs extra staff resources. The BA on our team has been tasked to build a baseline understanding of how many staff members are currently engaged in this activity, and how many would be required to do it at a 'best practice' level. This sounds simple, but is proving very difficult as many people in this organization do many tasks, so the BA is finding it hard to get concrete information on who does what, and for how much of their time. We spend our 'problem solving' time on two issues: First we debate the actual methodology he is using to get the information—is he asking the right questions? Are the answers he's getting going to tell us what we need to know? Is there a better way of approaching this issue?

Second we lay out the PowerPoint pages that we'll use at the end of this process to tell the story of what we have found. This is a common way of working, to start with 'ghost pages' that we think we'll end up using, then to gradually fill them in with information as the study progresses. This way everyone on the team, including the partners, can get engaged from the beginning in both the 'what' and the 'how' of what is being worked on, rather than having it all in the head of the person doing the analysis until the last minute. We find that drawing out the pages on a whiteboard throws up a number of questions that mean we have to re-evaluate the actual methodology, and this in turn changes the pages we think we'll end up with. In this way, we gradually iterate our way towards something we're happy with. At this point we get the Engagement Manager in and talk her through our thinking. She too has questions, and we spend another half an hour iterating further until we are all convinced that we've got it right.

1:45 p.m. The lead partner on our project has been in a meeting with the Chief Executive, and now has fifteen minutes free before he has to head back to the office, so we all head out to grab some lunch. We choose sushi (London seems to be experiencing a sushi boom at the moment) and end up sitting on a wall on a quiet residential backstreet, enjoying the sunshine and talking about our summer holidays.

2:00 p.m. After the success of the top team workshop, one of the directors has asked us to run a similar workshop for his department. The difference with this one is that I'll be leading it. For the top team workshop, the Engagement Manager and I prepared the materials, and worked with the partners on the facilitation guide for the day. We then attended the day, taking notes and helping out where required, while the partners led the actual activities. For this next workshop, however, it turns out that all the partners, as well as the Engagement Manager, will be presenting a paper at an international conference and will be unable to attend, so this will be up to me. Needless to say, this is quite a challenge for me and I have a few butterflies, as well as a lot of excitement, at the prospect. Right now we have a meeting with the director and two of his staff. The Engagement Manager and I lay out our initial thoughts for the day, and listen to their ideas. Together, we combine our ideas, creating some new potential activities, and end up with a plan that we are all happy with. At the end of the meeting, they mention that this workshop will be taking place at a hotel outside of London, and that they will all be staying there the night before. They invite me to join them for the night before and I accept their invitation—it will be a great opportunity to get to know them socially before the day itself.

3:15 p.m. As we didn't have any more client meetings scheduled, we have relocated back to our office at Piccadilly Circus. Other than writing up my notes from the previous meeting and creating a new plan for the workshop, I am free until 5, so decide to squeeze in a session at the gym.

3:30 p.m. My New Year's Resolution, almost nine months ago, was to get to the gym at least once a week. Since we have a gym at our office there really isn't any excuse. It took me until June to venture in there, but recently I've been managing to get in at least once a week. Today I ask the instructor for a tutorial on how to use the rowing machine properly. I find out what I had suspected, that my amateurish efforts weren't the correct way to use the machine, but at least now I know.

4:45 p.m. A quick call with my wife to say hi.

5:00 p.m. I have a meeting with the communication specialist assigned to our team. He is an expert in designing and running workshops, among other things, and we talk through my thoughts for the workshop I will be running. He has difficulty understanding one of the games I have created, so he makes me stand up and talk him through it—exactly what I'll say and exactly what I want everyone to do. This certainly focuses me on the pros and cons of what I've been thinking about. We find some problems and talk them through, and in the end design a game that we are both really excited about. Most importantly, he also agrees to accompany me to the workshop and to co-host with me. We will tag-team, taking it in turns to run a session. It is good to know I'll be able to draw on his experience and have something of a 'safety net'.

6:00 p.m. We have a team meeting in the lead partner's office. As well as our core team of three and the lead partner, we have two other partners closely involved with this study, so there are 6 of us gathered round a conference table, each with a print out of a PowerPoint document in front of us. We are talking through a meeting we will be having with the Chief Executive and the leadership team tomorrow morning. We'll be taking them through what we have found so far, and what we think the next steps should be. We'll be using a PowerPoint pack to guide the meeting, so now we are talking through this document. There is some disagreement about one of the priority areas that was raised in the previous workshop, both in terms of how we present the outcome of the workshop, and what we think they should do as a result. We end up redesigning a number of key pages in the PowerPoint pack, and agree that with these changes done we should be in good shape for the meeting tomorrow. The result is that the core team will have to edit the PowerPoint this evening and send it out to the partners to read tonight.

6:50 p.m. A quick call home to talk to my daughters and say goodnight to them. I tell my wife it looks like I'll be home at a fairly sensible time today.

7:15 p.m. The EM, the BA and I have a quick huddle to ensure that we all have the same understanding of what we just agreed. We work at a whiteboard and draw out the new slides, debating each one until we are happy. When each one is finished, we print out a copy, scan it, and email it to our visual graphics production office in India. They will produce the slides and send them back ASAP.

8:00 p.m. The slides have all gone out to India (we have an outsourcing center there that prepares PowerPoint slides from drafts), and we agree to call it a day. The finished slides will come back by the time we have got home, and we'll each check the produced versions, and then send them to the EM, who will collate them and send them out to the partners. As a final end of day 'ritual', we sit down in three bizarrely designed chairs (they look like donuts on legs, and it is not at all clear how how I to sit on them!) in a corner of our open plan office. We spend 5 minutes on a team 'check-out', referring back to the goals we'd discussed at the beginning of the day, and talking about whether or not we've achieved them. Everyone has had a successful day, so we say goodnight and head off home.

9:00 p.m. After another 22 minutes reading on the train, and the short drive back to my village, I'm home. I open the laptop and log on to the network. The pages are back from India, so I check them against the paper printouts, make some small adjustments, and send them on to the Engagement Manager.

9:10 p.m. Dinner with my wife at home.

9:30 p.m. Sitting on the couch with a beer, watching an episode of The West Wing. We didn't catch it when it was on TV, and lots of our friends recommended it, so now the adventures of President Bartlett and his team are in danger of overtaking our life!

10:10 p.m. The episode finishes, and my wife and I look at each other, then at the tv. We are both thinking the same thing. Time for one more episode!

Conclusions about what a consulting day might commonly include:

From these two examples we can begin to see some themes emerging. Of course, every project is different, and every consultant will have a different experience, but most will agree with the following list:

- PowerPoint. Lots of PowerPoint.
- Internal team meetings, where work is assigned and/or reviewed

- Partner meetings, where a senior consultant reviews the team's work and offers additional perspective and challenge (also 'causing' additional work!)
- Client meetings – sometimes to gather information, sometimes to show them the work so far
- More PowerPoint.
- Logistical stuff like travelling from A to B, scheduling and eating meals

Working hours:
- Almost always at least 10 hours a day (e.g., 9 'til 7), often 12 (e.g., 8 'til 8 or 9 'til 9), and fairly frequently a lot more (basically, you should be prepared to be working all the time you are awake during the week – although not weekends)

Travel
- For many of the large companies, and many of the smaller ones as well unless they state otherwise, you should also assume that you might need to be out of town sometimes. Some projects and clients this will be Mon thru Thu every week, other times it will be more sporadic.

Work/Life
- Putting the two things above together, you should realize that the things that many 'normal' people do during their evenings are not open to you. For instance, you can't sign up to be in an amateur dramatic performance. You can't join a soccer league that plays every Wednesday evening. You can't promise your spouse you'll always do the grocery shopping on Tuesday evening. This is definitely a downside of consulting.

How does the job evolve over time?
The scenarios I've described above, and many of the experiences you will hear from alumni who graduated within the last couple of years,

refer to the 'MBA entry level' position. This is the part of the hierarchy where you are, for the most part, the foot soldier, the 'front line' team member who is gathering information, running analysis, making PowerPoint pages, and making more PowerPoint pages.

In some firms, you will also be managing more junior consultants. In others you'll wait a while before you get to manage.

After the entry level stage, there are two positions of note. Many companies have further divisions, but these are the two that really stand out:

- Manager
- Partner

Manager

As a project manager, you are the person who is at the center of a network that includes junior consultants, partners, and clients. You may be the most senior person who is staffed full time to the project, and you may be the consultant that spends most time, day to day, with the client.

Being a project manager at a consulting company, you will get a lot of training and experience at project management (sounds obvious doesn't it!) – this is a very useful skill in a lot of other walks of life.

You also get experience at managing, coaching and teaching junior staff. Sometimes you will get training in how to do this, and sometimes you will design your style on ways that you yourself were managed.

In addition, you will get a lot of exposure to more senior consultants (partners) and you will start to learn what being a partner involves. If you decide you want to move on to that level, you will start to do the things that partners do, including developing client relationships, 'winning' work and perhaps getting involved in the internal management of the consulting company.

Partner

A partner at a consulting company (often a part-owner or a shareholder) is the person on a specific project who is responsible for delivering the work. She will probably be the 'owner' of the client relationship, and will often also be an expert in the industry or function in which she works. She will spend a lot of her time overseeing current work – meeting with the teams she has deployed to ensure they are on track, as well as a lot of time developing new work – either cultivating existing relationships or developing new ones.

As a partner, this person will also take a close interest, and probably some degree of day to day role, in the internal management of the consulting company. This may cover such things as recruiting, operations, finance, marketing etc.

One thing I'd say is true about my friends who are partners at consulting firms is that they are passionate about what they do. (You have to be to have made a success of a job that is such a lot of work.) They earn a lot of money and spend a lot of their time surrounded by many of the things that success brings. They also work on exciting projects and advise top leaders of top organizations, so they can really feel that they are at the heart of exciting and important decisions. On the other hand they don't get to spend a lot of time during the week doing anything else (e.g., spending time with their family, or any of the other hobbies or pastimes that other people might take for granted). Hence the need for passion for the job.

What are the pros and cons of being a consultant?

This section (perhaps even more so than the others) is going to revolve around my personal opinions, and I'll additionally bring in the many conversations I have had over the years with colleagues and classmates, both while I was a consultant and since then.

What's best about being a consultant?

You frequently move from one project to another

Many people who like consulting point to the fact that they are the type of person who gets bored easily, loves novelty, and loves new challenges. Other types of people would hate this – having to learn new things every few weeks or months, teams being shuffled around, offices being changed and so on.

You are given frequent feedback and training, so you learn really quickly

It is amazing how quickly you can advance in a skill if each time you do something you are given closely observed feedback and training on how to get better. Furthermore, each time you get comfortable at something, you will be pushed to the next level. This can be scary but also exhilarating.

Your achievements are closely monitored, and rewarded

Before I was a consultant, when I was working for myself, I would sometimes sit at my desk very late at night and wish that there was someone who would walk by, notice how hard I was working, and say 'well done'. You definitely get that in consulting, and if you put in the effort, and produce high quality work, somebody will notice.

You work with really clever and hard-working colleagues

It's very exciting and reassuring to know that everyone you work with is as smart, motivated and hard-working as you are. When you leave consulting, you will find a much wider variety of skill and effort amongst your future colleagues, and it will be more difficult to get things done!

Many of the skills you learn are very valuable in many other jobs

It sounds trivial, but a lot of what you learn as a consultant is about the basics of 'doing business' – stuff like how to run a meeting or a phone call, how to put a project together and manage it efficiently, how to give someone feedback. These are the tools of the trade for a consultant, and they are tools that will serve you well for the rest of your career.

You earn a lot of money

When you graduate, chances are you need to earn some serious money to start paying back your loans. Consulting is reasonably well paid, by which I mean you won't get as much as classmates who go into banking, but you'll make a lot more than people in most other industries, particularly at your level of experience. There aren't many jobs where you can get a sigificant salary for doing something you have absolutely no experience doing!

You often get to work on things that are 'important'

Consulting is a great way to feel like you are at the heart of important stuff. Perhaps you will end up working on something that will be on the front page of the newspaper, or respectfully referred to by Governments, or may contribute to the well-being of people. As I've said already, consultants are expensive, and so are usually only hired when the problem is extreme.

What's worst about being a consultant?

You work a lot of long hours

This is without a doubt the most significant drawback of being a consultant (assuming that consistently working long hours is a negative for you, some people are hard-wired to like it). There's no getting round it, consulting is a full-time occupation, and by that I mean you should really consider yourself at work for all the hours you are awake between Monday morning and Friday evening. Some companies and some locations extend this into (and sometimes through) the weekend. Make sure you find out about the company and office location you are considering and go into the job with your eyes open.

You don't have control over your time

Working long hours is not the end of the world by itself, in fact it may be just what you are looking for. The harder part of the equation is that you generally don't have much control over that busyness. At a junior level, your time is usually controlled by your manager and the partners in your team. Even at a senior level, you are essentially at the whim of your clients, so that if they suddenly want something done by 8am Monday morning, your weekend plans may have to be put on hold.

You usually move on, just as the implementation is about to get going

This is probably the answer that most consultants give when asked why they left, and they don't want to appear 'wimpy' by complaining about the workload. And it's true, it is frustrating to put in a lot of work into designing something, and then have to step out just as it is about to be implemented. Clearly this will change if you take one of the more recently developed 'implementation' roles or work at a firm where implementation is a focus.

You get a lot of feedback

I still wince when I hear the phrase 'can I give you some feedback'! When you are working in an environment where you are constantly learning, constantly being challenged, and constantly being told how you can improve, it can get to the point where sometimes you just want to be left alone for a while! Being continually told how you could have done something better can sometimes have the unfortunate effect that you start to doubt your abilities to a serious extent. I've seen many people who were naturally very self-confident be reduced to quivering wrecks by too much negative feedback. In order to survive this and thrive you need to be able to keep in touch with your own sense of value and worth, and be able to take the feedback in the spirit in which it was intended, not giving it the power to sap your energy too much.

Your friends and colleagues frequently leave the company

When I joined McKinsey, there was a group of people who I really liked and identified with. The fact that they worked there was a major part in my decision to join the firm. By the time I left, none of them were still there, and many of the people I'd got to know during my time there had also left. (To counter that, many other great people I met along the way are still there). It can be dispiriting and lonely sometimes to realize that a lot of your friends have moved on, especially when it seems like every Friday brings another 'I'm leaving' email. This is an inevitable part of working in a company where the average length of stay is less than five years, and perhaps this is part of the culture now for many non-consulting companies (certainly the age of having a job for life has well and truly passed).

Getting an interview

Getting a job is essentially a two-step process – first you need to get an interview (not a trivial task), and then you need to succeed in that interview (or series of interviews).

So let's start by looking at how you can get that interview.

This is the only major point where the process and experience will be very different depending on your current situation. Let's say there are a number of categories:

- You are (or are about to be) a student (undergrad or MBA) at a 'core' school
- You are (or are about to be) a student (undergrad or MBA) at a non-core school
- You are not at school, you are already working, and you'd like to transition into consulting
- You are in a senior position, with many years of expertise, and you'd like to transition into consulting

I've put them into this order because I think that is the order of relevance to most of the people who are going to be using this book.

Most of what I talk about in this chapter is going to be directly relevant for category 1, useful for category 2, and of interest but not directly relevant to the others.

Before I proceed I'll quickly cover the other categories, in reverse order.

If you are a senior expert, with a great network, it is possible that you might be able to go straight into a consulting company, perhaps even as a partner. Clearly this kind of transition is going to be on a case by case basis, and unfortunately this part of this book isn't going to be of much use. I still believe the rest of it will be helpful in terms of understanding what goes on behind the scenes at your target company. Your best route is going to be your network – perhaps you have engaged or worked with consultants in the past. Hopefully someone in your network can set up a conversation for you with a partner at a firm. Failing that, an executive search firm would be a good starting place. Experienced headhunters will have a good idea of what consulting firms are looking for, and will be able to give good perspective on whether you fit the bill.

If you are not a senior expert, but have built up considerable work experience, then you would be considered an 'experienced' or 'lateral' hire. Many consulting companies have dedicated channels set up for this kind of recruiting. Common ways into this channel might be:

- Recommendation from someone in your network who works at the company
- Recommendation from a headhunter
- Cold call – certainly at the bottom of the list but not to be discounted – perhaps you will call up the company, ask to speak to someone in recruiting who deals with lateral hires, and find out what their process is and whether you could be considered.

As we discussed earlier in the section about implementation, probably the most promising way in to a consulting company nowadays, for someone with industry experience, is to join a firm as either an industry specialist or an implementation specialist. For either of these routes, the first step is to network your way to someone in the firm who either works in the relevant practice, or recruits for it.

Networking in this context is something that strikes fear into the hearts of a lot of people. The idea of reaching out to people you don't know, and asking them for help, can seem daunting.

My best advice if you find yourself in this situation, is to get hold of a copy of Steve Dalton's excellent book on networking, 'The Two Hour Job Search'. The title sounds a bit gimmicky, and of course succeeding in a job search like this will take a lot more than two hours, but the content is excellent – a thorough examination of what works when building a professional network and activating that network to help you get a job interview. I recommend it to all of the students and experienced hires I work with.

So that leaves categories 1 and 2 – students at a core or non-core school.

What does it mean to be a core school, why do companies have such distinctions, and why do they put such an effort into having a presence at such places?

What is a 'core school'

A core school is a school that the consulting company will use as an important and recurring source of hiring. Because of this, there will be a committed group of alumni of the school at the company, and these alumni will often be the driving force behind the recruiting effort.

Recruiting at a core school will be a well-defined process. To a certain extent, if you are a student at such a school you can let the process come to you. If you are outside of this set of schools you will need to do some more work to get on the radar of your target company.

Why do companies have core schools?

One of the most difficult challenges a consulting company faces is to find a continual supply of talented and hard-working consultants. Business schools and top undergrad institutions are a great place to find people with the right combination of skills, including:

- Intelligence
- Passion for solving problems
- Drive to work hard and succeed

Even better, leading schools already employ rigorous screening procedures, so graduates are already 'pre-approved'.

If I own a consulting company, and I want people with the above skills, the easiest and most efficient place for me to go find them is at a top Business School.

Similarly, if I want the cleverest, most hard-working and driven undergrads, I'll go to the top Universities in the World – places where just to have got admitted proves you may well have what I'm looking for.

In other words, I'll fish where the fish are.

If you are an undergrad or MBA student at a non-core school

First it helps to be aware of the recruiting calendar that the companies use for their core schools, because if you do manage to get into that process, you will probably still be part of the same timeline. So any research you can do that will get you that information will be invaluable – perhaps you have a friend at a core school, or perhaps you can find material online about that school. Very often if you go to a company website you can access pages that are specific to a core school, either if you are not attending it. For instance, at joinbain.com, you can select 'your school' and type in any top B school – then you can see the information that is available to students of that school. A lot of it will not be relevant, but the general information, including the calendar, will be helpful.

Second, you need to find a way in. As with number 3 above, there is always the cold call to the recruiting team, and this may work, but ideally you would have some kind of personal connection.

- Is there anyone you know at all who works at your target company?
- Even a second connection on LinkedIn?
- Has an alum of your university or school ever worked at the company?

Don't be shy to use your network. It proves that you are passionate about the company. Sometimes it may turn out to be a dead end, but hopefully during the process you will have made, or re-kindled, some useful connections. If the target company doesn't work out, perhaps go back through your contacts and ask if they can think of any other companies you could try.

If you are an undergrad or MBA student at a 'core' school

Getting an interview with a consulting company that recruits on campus is a fairly well defined process. At its most basic, there will be a time (for instance, November or December for MBA intern applications at US Business Schools) when you apply. The application will most likely be online and will consist of your resume, perhaps a cover letter, and perhaps some additional information. The company will review these applications and pick who to interview. If there is a bid system, you can also use this as a second chance to get the interview.

Sounds simple, and actually in terms of logistics it is.

So what about all of the events that come before the application deadline? Opportunities including company briefings, treks, coffee chats, office hours, informational phone calls... the list goes on...

For the most part, the many events during this period (Fall term for many MBAs) are for your benefit, to allow you to get to know the company.

They are also, however, a chance for the company to get to know you, so that when your application does arrive in their system in November, they have perhaps already built a hypothesis about whether you are someone they want to interview.

This reciprocal process of you getting to know them, and them getting to know you, is called networking. Note that this isn't strictly the same kind of networking as in other settings, where your relationship building is long-term. This is quite a short term, fairly transactional type of networking that to all concerned is built around the common goal of finding out if you might be a good fit for the company in a fairly limited amount of time.

Let's start by reviewing some of the basics of on-campus recruiting, and then spinning through the main events, with the goal of finding out how you can use these networking opportunities to maximize your chance of getting on the interview list.

We'll look at the following topics:

On-campus recruiting
- What does on-campus recruiting involve?
- What does the process look like from the company's perspective?
- Closed lists and Open lists

Networking
- Do I really need to network for consulting?
- What does good networking look like?
- How should I make the best use of the company briefing and ensuing cocktail reception?
- How should I make the best use of a small event like a dinner?
- How should I make the best use of a one on one meeting?
- How should I reach out to alumni?
- How should I think about the recruiter compared to the consultants?

On-Campus Recruiting

For a large company, recruiting at a core school may involve keeping an office onsite, perhaps staffed by an 'ambassador' – a consultant who has been temporarily staffed to the school office, where his/her job will be primarily to market the company to students, and to get to know students so that the company can be sure they are picking the right people to interview.

In addition, there may be a dedicated website, and other online features.

For actual recruiting, at a core school, a large company will have a complete program of marketing and recruiting activities – during a typical first year, it may look something like this:

Summer (before students arrive) – offer students the opportunity to attend **pre-MBA program.**

September – **company briefing** (PowerPoint presentation to any interested students), probably followed by a **cocktail reception.**

October – further **targeted events** (perhaps a winetasting evening, or a dinner at a local restaurant.) These may be invite-only, based on the results of networking or the company having read through the school's resume book. Perhaps an opportunity to **visit the local office** of the company.

November– **coffee chats** and **office hours** (usually one on one opportunities to sit down with a consultant and get to know them and their company). **Case workshop** followed by chance to do individual **practice cases** with consultants.

December – **application deadline** for summer internship.

January – more **case practice**, followed by **on-campus interviews**. Sometimes these on-campus interviews will encompass first and decision rounds.

February – perhaps **second round interviews** at the relevant office (in which case companies pay to fly students to the office where they want to work).

For a small company, the events may be a subset of the above.

What does the process look like from the company's perspective?

Let's look at on campus recruiting from the point of view of a recruiter, looking at a core Business School. Here's what their timeline might look like:

September: Resume screen and company briefing
- Buy access to the resume book.
  - Review all resumes and look for candidates who meet your criteria.
  - Develop a long-list of potential candidates, probably with some of the students at the top of the list marked out as being of particular interest.

- Begin on-campus activity with company briefing and open reception.
  - Send a team of consultants (many of whom will be alumni of the school) to present the briefing and host the reception.
  - Collect impressions from consultants after the reception (they will probably meet too many people to give detailed reports, but some students may stand out either positively or negatively).

October and November: Host events, and gather impressions of students
- Run events.
  - You may host an office visit, where students will get the chance to drop by, meet more of your consultants, and see where you work. This is also a great way for you to judge which students are interested (for instance, when you print out a set of nametags for those who have signed up, it's easy to look at the table at the end of the event and see which students didn't show up).
  - Perhaps you will use your long-list to decide which students to invite to targeted events such as small dinners.

- Maintain database of first hand impressions.
  - As consultants get more contact with students, either through smaller events or through individual outreach

by students, ensure to collect feedback so that the long-list of candidates can be adjusted.

December: Receive applications and make decisions about who to Interview

- Review cover letters and resumes, comparing them to information you have already gathered.

  (As you can see, at this point the 'job application' is the first time the student has officially applied, but it is certainly not the first time that the company has thought about the student.)

  - For some candidates, the recruiter may chase up consultants who have met the student, and ask for more detailed impressions.

- Decide who to interview.
  - This is a big decision – a company will only have a limited number of interview slots, compared to the number of applicants.
  - If you are a recruiter, your biggest fear is that you are missing out on a star.
  - You also don't want to waste your consultants' time by making them interview someone who is clearly not going to make it.
  - Finally, you have to consider the issue of yield – if you make 80 interview offers, not all 80 students will take up the offer (some of them may have decided not to go for consulting for instance).

January : Ensure support for those you have chosen

- You've chosen your students, now you want to get a good crop of offers.
  - Perhaps you will set up each applicant with a 'buddy' to ensure that they have someone to talk to during the stressful and sometimes confusing interview process.

- Perhaps you will decide to give extra help in terms of case practice, especially to those students you truly believe you want. After all, you've spent a lot of time and money in the last six months finding and developing these 'leads'. It's in your interest to get a good return from that investment.

It seems like the recruiter is incentivized to hire people and will give 'interesting' candidates a lot of help and access – doesn't this skew the system unfairly?

Firstly, fair has got nothing to do with it.

Secondly, (and less flippantly), it's true that the recruiter's job is to hire people. It's also true that while you are going through the process it can seem like some people are getting more attention than others. Some parts of that process are not 'fair', and that's just life. If a candidate has a resume that screams out 'I'd make a great consultant', and if that candidate also has great people skills and can network really well, then yes that candidate is going to get more 'love' from the company.

But the recruiter only has limited power, because the hiring decision will involve many other people

> All of this 'love' will not get someone hired. Having said all of the above about fairness, perhaps the best thing about consulting recruiting is that the interview process itself is entirely fair. If you nail the interview, they'll hire you. If you don't, they won't. It doesn't matter how many dinners you attended, or how many networking conversations you knocked out of the park – if you can't pass through all of the many parts of the interview process, you don't get in.

Closed lists and Open lists

The process I've described above shows how a company develops its list of students to interview. This is known as a **closed list**, because the company controls it entirely.

Some schools also have a process to get an interview with the company that works alongside the closed list. This is known as an **open list**. For instance, at Tuck, the company can only choose 50% of the students that it will interview. The other 50% of interview slots are 'auctioned' to the students in a fair system that starts by giving all students the same number of points, then allows students to 'bid' for interviews across all the companies who are recruiting. When you are choosing a Business School, find out if they have a system like this. Perhaps you don't need it because you are confident you'll get on the closed list. But perhaps you feel that your resume might not tell a compelling enough story because you are a career switcher, and perhaps you feel that the only way you can truly get your story across is in an interview, not a fairly awkward networking event where you are competing for attention with a lot of other students. Either way, you should make your decision based on knowledge about this system, not find out about it when it's too late.

Why do companies allow some schools to run an open list?

For some schools it may simply be part of the price of recruiting there.

Many companies would, if given the choice, select a closed list process. But actually many recruiters will admit that their process for selecting closed list candidates (resume screening, networking etc.), is far from perfect. Having a portion of interviews go to those students who are most passionate (shown by the amount of points they bid) is actually a great way to ensure a company is not missing out on someone they really ought to interview.

Finally, remember what I said about the alumni being a key part of recruiting. It may well be the case that a senior partner at the company got their break many years ago by getting onto the open list. Hopefully that person has a fairly charitable view towards the open list concept!

I have a friend who is a very successful consultant – he got his interview because a couple of hours beforehand another student pulled out, and my friend managed to run home, get his suit and tie, and take the vacated spot. You can be sure he keeps an open mind when a student gets a last minute interview slot with him!

Networking

Our overview of on-campus recruiting included a large number of events that invariably generate a lot of questions from incoming students. Let's look at some of these frequently asked questions, particularly with regard to networking, in more detail:

- Do I really need to network for consulting?
- What does good networking look like?
- How should I make the best use of the company briefing and ensuing cocktail reception?
- How should I make the best use of a small event like a dinner?
- How should I make the best use of a one on one meeting ?
- How can I reach out to alumni?
- How should I think about the recruiter compared to the consultants?

Do I really need to network for consulting?

Many students pick up on the idea that for investment banking jobs, there is a lot of networking required (for instance, multiple trips to Manhattan to visit banks). They also hear that this is not true for consulting, or perhaps there is a different (lower) level of networking that might be required.

So what's the answer?

The short answer is that yes, you do need to network with consultants in order for them to build an understanding of who you are. It is also true that this networking may be far less intense than that experienced by your classmates who are looking for banking jobs.

As you saw from the process above (and this is particularly crucial if you are only able to get to interview via a closed list), a company may form an initial impression of you from your resume. There are a number of other 'formal' opportunities during the year to add to that impression, starting with perhaps a brief chat after a company briefing, or a well-thought question during the office visit. It is entirely possible to make a good enough impression to get on a closed list just from these small interactions.

> *A senior partner at a small consulting firm said that once you have met him, and made a good impression on him, that's enough – you don't need to systematically work your way through every member of his firm.*

Indeed, as we learnt from the recruiter process above, many firms will make an effort to track and centralize the results of their networking with you.

Perhaps my favorite advice is from another manager, at another top firm.

> *"In every interaction with our company, you are either gaining or losing share. Therefore you should be mindful of the fact that each time you meet with us there is a risk that you undo some of the good work you have already done."*

To conclude: Yes, you should network. Yes, that networking is less intense than it is for banking. Be aware that not all networking is successful, and that you might be 'losing share' compared to a fellow student who had her one successful networking moment then knew when to call it a day.

What does good networking look like?

This is what, when I was a consultant, I would have called 'the killer question' – meaning this is the question that if we can answer, we'll be a long way to solving all of our problems.

I'll start by stating my overall thoughts on what good networking looks like. Then I'll spend a bit of time elaborating.

Good networking involves the following:

- Getting to know somebody, and having them get to know you, so that from now on you are no longer strangers
- Letting the other person know what you are looking for
- If the other person is a recruiter, giving that person enough information to allow them to make their own decision about whether you might be someone they should be interested in
- Keeping track of the relationship

Networking does NOT involve the following

- Selling
- Persuading
- Convincing
- Pitching
- Acting
- Pretending to be somebody other than your true self

There are probably whole shelves full of books about networking, but I think the problem with a lot of networking theory, and certainly with the way that many of us think of networking, is that it focuses on *building a relationship with the intent to sell something or asking for something.*

Many people hate the idea of having to sell something. They conjure up images of 'used car salesmen', people forcing a shabby product on a customer who doesn't really want it, but succumbs due to the persistence or magnetism of the sales person.

As I mentioned earlier, I'm an introvert. That means that the idea of walking into a room full of people I don't know makes me nervous. Very nervous.

If you then told me that I didn't just have to go into that room to hang out, I had to go into there and 'sell something', I'd freeze. Every muscle in my body would tense up. My heart would start pounding. My palms would get sweaty. My breathing would get heavy. In short, it wouldn't be a pretty sight! It certainly wouldn't get me in the right state of mind to go and meet people who need to get a good impression of me!!

So trust me when I say this:

At no point in your job search are you going to sell anything to anyone.

Relax. Breathe. Accept what I'm telling you, and stop trying to 'sell yourself'!

Let's think this through for a second, because very often books throw around pieces of advice like this that sound good the instant you read them, yet don't pass muster when you think through the implications. So allow me to push a bit further on this idea.

I think we can agree on the following points:

Consulting companies want to hire MBA students. If they didn't, they wouldn't come to campus or post job opportunities.

Consulting companies know what type of person they want.
They've been doing this for years, and they've developed it into a science.

You either are or you aren't that person. Sounds harsh, but there it is. As I said earlier, you either have the competencies and personality they want, or you don't. If you don't, it's conceivable you could 'act', but you'd end up getting a job you'd be miserable in.

If we accept the above points, I think we should conclude the following:

You want the company to get to know you, so they can decide for themselves if you are the type of person they want.

Here's a more advanced point, that isn't obvious to you as a student:

The company only has limited resources to interview students, and it wants to get a good yield from that process, therefore they are also trying to find out who is truly interested, compared to who is just 'window-shopping'. If everyone they interviewed turned out to be really interested in Wall St. instead, they'd have wasted their effort. A win for a consulting company is that it only interviews people who are sure they want to be consultants, and even better are sure they want to work for that company.

So we should also conclude:

You want the company to know that you are interested in consulting, not just a random Wall St. guy who showed up for a free drink. Even better, if you are passionate about that particular company, let them know.

If networking isn't selling, what is it?

At the risk of laboring this point, I'm going to suggest a different analogy in order to get the 'used car salesman' out of our head once and for all.

You want to buy an iPhone or an iPad. You know the price, and frankly price is not part of your buying decision. You want it because it fits in with your needs, and you know beyond a doubt that it is an Apple device that you want.

There is an Apple store next to your office, so you are also in no doubt about where you will buy this device. Since Apple ensures that its devices are the same price no matter where you buy them from, there is absolutely no downside to walking into the store and picking your device.

You walk into the store. You have your credit card with you. You are ready to buy.

But you do have some questions – which model do you really want? You know how you think you'll use it – mostly web surfing at home, some email, some music etc. You know there are a variety of models, each one with a variety of options – storage, screen resolution, size, weight, etc.

A sales associate walks up to you and offers some help.

You tell her that you know that you want a device, you just want some help understanding which device would be the best for you.
Imagine you are that sales associate. Do you think the next five minutes is going to be stressful or enjoyable? You are going to talk about things you are passionate about, and at the end of the conversation, the customer will go away happy. Do you think you are going to have to do any 'selling'?

When you walk into a networking event, you are the Apple sales associate. Recruiters are there because they have already decided they need to hire some students from your school. They already have a very good understanding of the type of work they'll want those students to do, and hence they have a very good understanding of what types of competencies they're looking for.

Do you think you're going to 'sell' them something they don't want? No.

You're going to let them know a little about yourself, and many other students will do the same. There will be more events like this. Then there will be interviews. At the end of all that, they will decide which iPod they want to buy. One last time – at no point in that process will they be 'persuaded' to 'buy' anything they don't want.

So – networking is allowing the other person to get to know you, to find out about your competencies, your passions, what you want out of life.

Keeping track

Keeping track of the relationship is vital.

During your MBA and onward career you'll meet a great many interesting people. You'll walk away from many interactions thinking to yourself – 'what an interesting person, I'll have to keep in touch'. Two days later the information about that person will have been over-written in your brain by all the other stuff that comes along. This is a problem for all of us.

Good networkers develop a system for keeping track. Some use dedicated software, some make an Excel spreadsheet, some write notes in a notepad, or on the back of business cards. Perhaps send a LinkedIn request (if you do this, ensure your profile is up to date and reflects what you want it to say about yourself for your current job search.) Don't send a Facebook friend request.

Whatever works for you, make sure you keep track. When you walk out of a cocktail event, make sure to take ten minutes to write down your notes. They may look like:

- Stephen Pidgeon. Engagement Manager. Wife and 2 daughters. Likes hiking and skiing. Talked about a project with a pharma client.
- John Doe. Senior partner. Spoke at presentation. Passionate about aviation. Based in Atlanta. Didn't speak with him (he was surrounded constantly) but he seemed really nice and said students are welcome to email him.
- Jane Smith. Second year student. Interned at BCG in Dallas office. Talked with her at dinner. Loves Glee and 30 Rock. Offered to help me with case practice.

How should I make the best use of the company briefing and ensuing cocktail reception?

A typical company briefing for a top consulting company may attract half the students in your class, or as many as the room can hold. It's largely a one sided presentation, where consultants stand in front of the auditorium with PowerPoint screens behind them, telling you about their company.

Is there anything you can do at such an event to gain or lose share?

First, let's start with the easier part of this

Is there anything you can do wrong that would hurt your chances of getting an interview?

Yes.

Let's look at a few examples. Most of these will seem so obvious to you that you will assume that only idiots would make these mistakes, but I promise you that these are all things that people do, largely because they stopped thinking that they were being evaluated, or because they were tired, or busy, or stressed.

Sitting with your laptop screen up, or checking your phone.
There's no more public and obvious way of signaling that you are not interested in a speaker than turning your eyes away and focusing on another screen.

I don't care if you are taking notes. Think for a second about what the person you're trying to impress might think. There are a hundred students watching him as if every word coming out of his mouth is gold, and then there are twenty others who are looking at a screen. Which are the ones he's going to feel he's making a real connection with? If you want to take notes, even if you don't, go in there with a notepad and pen and write down what these guys are saying. It will be helpful to you, and it shows you are interested.

Turning up early, but choosing to sit at the back
I know that there are times when you arrive at an event and the only available seats are at the back – in that case, take them.

If there are seats available at the front, no matter what time you turn up, take them. What more obvious signal that you are super interested in this presentation could you send? *I know there's a basic human aversion to sitting at the front. Get over it.*

Actually, turning up early gives you the best chance to say hi to the consultants. After the event there will be a mad rush for the front. Before the event, people come in, nervously take a seat, and avoid eye contact. Why the difference? I don't know the answer, but I do know that this is a situation you can take advantage of – be the student who comes to the front, and makes a point of saying hi, even engaging in some light conversation.

Leaving early

I told you there'd be things here that are so obvious you'll cringe. This is one of those. But still people do it. Imagine you are a senior partner of a consulting company. You've given up a significant portion of your very valuable time to come and present to a large group of students. Three quarters of the way through the presentation, someone gets up, grabs their stuff, pushes their way past everyone else in the row, and leaves via a door that then bangs loudly behind them. If I were that partner, I'd make a point of giving one of my team the job of finding out who that person was, so I could make sure not to have them on my interview list.

If you have to leave, sit next to the door. When you leave through that door, treat it like any sound it makes is deadly – close it like it is made of fragile glass.

Asking stupid questions

I thought long and hard about using the word stupid here. I know you wouldn't set out to ask a stupid question. But I have to tell you, from the perspective of the presenter, they really do get asked.

What constitutes a stupid question?

- Something that was answered in the presentation that shows you clearly weren't listening.
- Something that could be answered by reading the main page of the company website.
- Something that only you would be interested in the answer to – remember you may be in a room with 100 other people, the consultants at the front don't want to spend 5 minutes answering a question that only helps you.

Asking questions that aren't questions

This is my personal gripe. It's not unique to company presentations, but will be found at any event where there is Q&A. Some wise-ass will raise their hand and start with a statement that attempts to show how clever they are, then talking for far too long, then finishing in a way that even the expert presenters don't know what to say. This leaves everyone else in the auditorium united in a common feeling of hatred. Don't be that person. Really.

So how can you 'gain share' at such an event?
There are a number of opportunities to make a good impression.

First, and this sounds obvious but most people don't do it, sit near the front, take out a notepad, and take notes. Listen carefully. Make eye contact. Nod when the presenter says something interesting. Laugh when they say something funny. Perhaps you've tried presenting to a large audience yourself. It's always reassuring to find a 'friend' in the audience – someone who seems to be in tune with what you are saying. If you as the presenter find this friend, you'll keep looking back to that person.

After the presentation there will be the Q&A opportunity. As discussed above, this is quite frequently a disaster area, filled with people losing share like you wouldn't believe. The safest option is to keep quiet. But there's always the possibility to stand out by asking a good question, particularly if you have already established a rapport with the presenter by sitting near the front and becoming his 'audience friend'.

What makes a good question?
There's no rule here, but I'm going to try to suggest some things that sound to me like they would be good questions.

- Something that shows you have done your homework, even before the company briefing. For instance, you might have read an article that the company recently published about an area that you are really interested in (let's say renewable energy). Assume they didn't cover this area during the presentation, you might let them know you read the article, and ask if this is a growth area for the company or if it was just a one-off piece of work.

- Something that shows you were really paying attention. One trick that consultants learn, and use, to show clients that they are really listening, is to paraphrase and repeat back what they have heard, along with a follow up question. A good consultant will often use this question to really provoke the client into thinking hard or reaching a new insight. So you could mirror this behavior and let them know that you too naturally act like a consultant. You could say, "Thinking back over the presentation, it felt like I heard a lot of your team talking around a common theme of passion for the client (this is the summary). How does that focus on the client actually play out? Is there ever a time when you have to weigh the interest of the client against the interest of your company, and if so, how do you make that call? (this is the challenging and interesting question)."

- The previous question is also an example of another promising category – the softball question about something you know the company likes to talk about. All consulting companies like to talk about how they serve clients, so in reality you're allowing the presenter a chance to talk for a couple of minutes about their distinctive client service. Another great softball question, and one that you really should want to know the answer to, is "how are consultants evaluated, and what happens if a consultant is identified as having a weakness?" Again, all consulting companies pride themselves on their professional development, including the ways they evaluate and train their consultants.

- Bearing in mind you want the presenters to remember you, and your question, another good type (although tricky) is one where you reveal information about yourself that you know they'll find memorable. I say this is tricky because you don't want this to come across as a blatant commercial for yourself. It helps if you have something fairly unique or memorable in your background. For instance, imagine if you were a presenter and a student asked "When I was coaching a team for the Olympics, I used to find myself struggling to find the right balance between pushing the team, and allowing them to find their own pace. Listening to your consultants, it sounds like they often experience the same dilemma between pushing each other for excellence and sometimes wanting to work at their own pace. How do you listen out for the warning signs that tell you if a team is being pushed too hard, and if you see that, how do you intervene?"

Aside from being a great softball question about the way that I, as a senior partner, like to ensure that none of my teams is pushing themselves so hard they are burning out, this is of course a great one that will ensure afterwards that the partner says to her assistant, 'find out the name of the guy who coached an Olympic team, we should keep an eye on him'.

- Finally, you can always fall back on the fact that people invariably love talking above themselves. You could, for instance, ask a senior partner about how they build long lasting relationships with clients. Or perhaps you could go personal, and ask them if when they themselves left Business School they ever imagined they'd still be consulting, so many years later. For a junior consultant, let them talk about something that makes them sound impressive. Perhaps ask them if they've formed their own client relationships yet, or ask them why they chose this company.

Finally, when the presentation ends, there's usually a point where the presenters are packing up their laptops and some students come down to the front to try and get some time with them.

Again, this is an opportunity to either gain or lose share. Bear in mind that after an hour long presentation, the presenter may be looking forward to a few moments to gather their thoughts. They may be checking their Phone, realizing how many important emails they've missed. They may be calling their car service to make sure that the car will be ready to pick them up. They may be talking with team members who they haven't had the chance to see for a year. So bear all of this in mind and don't just charge in, expecting that talking with you is at the top of their priority list.

On the other hand, perhaps the presenter is making signs that he or she is looking for feedback or validation from the audience. Perhaps they are not checking their device, but are looking out at the students. Best practice here is to approach the presenter or one of the team, shake their hand, introduce yourself, let them know how much you loved their presentation, and ask if they'd mind if you sent a follow up email with a couple of questions that the presentation has inspired. If you have a business card, hand it over, then thank them again, and leave. Show them that you respect their time, that you don't want to stop other students from meeting them, and that you have also got important things to be doing yourself. If you went from opening to closing handshake in 30 seconds then walked confidently away, you'd be in really good shape.

The cocktail reception, and the circle of death

Very often, after the company briefing, the consultants and students will move to an area that has been laid out with a bar and lots of space for people to stand around and talk to each other. Sometimes there will be food.

First of all, I'm going to tell you what this experience is like for a consultant. This is based on my own experience at a number of top Business Schools. I'm going to perhaps err on the side of negativity.

Here's what I often experienced:

> We'd do the presentation. Sometimes I'd speak. Sometimes I was a supporting character, lining the back of the stage. After the presentation we'd get swarmed by students. At some point

we'd get directed to the cocktail reception. I'd enter the reception area and make a beeline for the bar. I'd also try to find the food, but often wouldn't succeed. I'd again get swarmed by students, and would end up with what consultants jokingly call 'the circle of death'. When a jokey title uses the word death, you can be sure it's not because it's referring to a pleasant experience for any concerned!

I'd stand in one spot for about an hour, often more, while student after student talked at me and asked me very basic questions. Very occasionally I'd find I was building a rapport with someone. Mostly it just felt like I was talking a lot. I'd very often get hoarse I was talking so much. I'd end up with about twenty business cards, and I'd give out a corresponding amount.

At the end of the evening, I'd notice that the food had all gone. The beer in my hand had gone warm and I hadn't had a chance to drink it. And then I had to leave, late in the evening, and make my way home where I would have to do the work I missed out on in the previous few hours.

The next time I wore that suit jacket I'd pull out a bunch of student business cards and put them in my drawer.

Later, a recruiter would ask me if I had any feedback on any of the candidates. Frankly it was usually very difficult to even remember who I'd spoken to, even with the help of the business cards. Sometimes I'd remember a particularly interesting, nice, or entertaining person. More often than not, I'd remember a bunch of basically nice people (whose names I couldn't recall), and a few who I really didn't get a good impression of, mainly because they monopolized the conversation for too long, or asked me stupid questions.

So...

First of all, bear in mind that a consultant is very busy. They do not get given time off to come to such events. If they have come, it is because they have probably used up some favors with their team, wrenched themselves away from work with the promise to catch up on it later in the evening, and rushed up to the event at the very last minute.

If you see a consultant checking her phone or making a call, give her some space. She'll be back with you shortly, but right now she needs to tend to 'the day job'.

This busy-ness probably also mean the consultant hasn't eaten for quite a while. You may find yourself in an area with a lavish amount of food. You may help yourself to this food. Please do. But also bear in mind that the consultant would love to get some of the food too. Perhaps you could even offer to walk the consultant over to the food, or to bring him some. Likewise with drinks.

So how can a student really make a good impression in the circle of death?

This is a tricky one. Most of the same rules apply as before, when we were talking about questions to ask at the briefing, although now the audience is smaller so you are allowed to ask things that might only apply to you.

There are a couple of golden rules here that I think we can set out. As with all rules, sometimes they may be broken, but you could do a lot worse than follow these:

Be brief!
If you are in a reception and there are ten consultants, the best thing you could do would be to aim for a few minutes with each of them, then leave. The same goes for other kinds of networking events. You're not here to build lifelong friendships, you're here to make a brief impression, find out if there's the start of a longer relationship, and above all impress them by showing that you can act in a professional and respectful way by respecting their own time. It's not rude to talk for

a few minutes, then politely thank the consultant for their time, give them a card, ask if you can get in touch in future with a follow up, and then walk away. If you really want brownie points, say you're heading to the bar and offer to get them a drink!!

Be positive!
The consultant is tired and is being asked the same thing by a hundred students. Actually that's not true. About fifty percent of the students are asking negative things such as "what's the latest time you ever left work?", "how do you feel when you're on a travel project and you can't see your wife and children from Monday thru Thursday?", or my personal peeve, anything that starts with "isn't it true that..." or uses a statistic, usually to prove that the company has some kind of hidden agenda to avoid hiring people from a specific country, to avoid hiring students from a particular school, or to give incoming consultants a hard time.

Wouldn't you rather be in the other fifty percent, who asks me something that allows me to smile, recall the good part of my job, and talk in an interesting way about something I love?

Look for some kind of connection!
It's a basic human thing. It's easier for us to get along if we find we have something in common. This is easier if I spoke at the presentation, because you can connect with something I said. Perhaps you are also married with children. Perhaps you went to the same undergrad school. Perhaps you previously worked at a client I mentioned.

Even better, if you had a chance to look me up on the alumni network, perhaps you found out something about me while I was at your university – maybe I played hockey, or lived in the same dorm as you.

And finally, the ABSOLUTE WINNER – send a thank you email the next day.
Remember I talked about arriving at the office the following day and emptying my pockets of business cards. It's very difficult to tell who was who.

The best way you can help a consultant remember the great conversation you had the evening before is to send a brief note thanking them for coming to your school, reminding them of what you talked about, perhaps reminding them of who you are. Consultants live and die by email, so once your mail is in your new friend's inbox, or filing system, you are now on their radar.

Even better, they might send a brief response to you. If you get this, hang on to it. When you want to get in touch again in a few weeks or months, you can simply reply to this email, and pick up the conversation, rather than essentially cold calling them.

How should I make the best use of a small event like a dinner?
The small-group dinner is a key part of the consulting company's arsenal. It's a great way for them to combine getting to know prospective candidates, and also impressing the candidates with their generosity. When you're a student, it's nice to be taken to a top restaurant, especially when a partner at a consulting firm is being generous with the wine list!

You might get invited to an event like this out of the blue, in which case something has presumably gone right in the process so far – perhaps the company picked you out of the resume book because you meet their criteria of 'interesting'. Perhaps you made a good impression at a previous networking event.

Alternately, you might have got onto this dinner via an open sign-up, or perhaps the company is literally working its way through the consulting club and it is your turn.

Based on what we have discussed so far, we can reiterate a couple of overall rules for getting the best out of the dinner:

- *Remember you are either gaining or losing share*

- *Be positive and enthusiastic*

- *Send a thank you note the next day*

Other than these rules, what's the big difference between a dinner and a cocktail event?

The main difference to my mind is the length of time that you are 'stuck' with someone, and they are 'stuck' with you. At a cocktail event it is perfectly acceptable, even desirable, to chat for a few minutes then politely move on. At a restaurant you might be sitting next to someone for a couple of hours. Even if the company makes an effort to move its staff around periodically, you're still going to be with the same person for 30 minutes or so.

So what will you talk about for this amount of time?
Bear in mind that there is a dual reason for this dinner

– first it's to 'sell' you on the idea of working for this company. For this, the consultants will be more than happy to talk about how great their job is. So think of lots of ways of asking them.

-second, it's to get to know you. So don't be afraid to talk about yourself. Bear in mind you want to show them that you are interesting, sociable, and interested in the sort of stuff they that too are interested in. A good way to start is with a question that you also have an opinion or some experience with. For instance, you could ask a consultant about the nicest hotel they've ever stayed in, and after they have finished you could share a few of your own hotel stories. Or you could ask them about the most challenging client they've worked with, and then share some examples of times when you too have had to deal with challenging clients. Play to your strengths.

I'm an introvert. I find small talk like this quite difficult. One of the most universally successful conversation topics I've found at many events like this is to get people talking about TV shows or movies. You could ask if they get time in the evenings to ever relax in the hotel room and actually watch TV – if so, what is their favorite show? As soon as you get into listing favorite shows, you'll find some common ground. For me it was often one of the big 'high quality' shows like The West Wing, The Wire etc. But the real bonding came when I found someone who liked one of the more 'silly' shows that I also love, like Ugly Betty or 30 Rock. You can do a similar thing with movies. If you have any other kind of passion, for instance if you absolutely love a particular sport/team/place, perhaps steer the conversation towards that. You don't want to be the person who made the whole night about themselves, but equally it's great to be able to write in your thank you email 'I was the guy who talked about getting chased by bears in Yosemite'.

Who will be doing most of the talking?

Very often there's a hierarchy at a dinner. If there's a partner, then often the junior consultants will defer to the partner, and will expect the partner to be the one regaling the table with war stories. Many partners are very good at this. Some are not. If you happen to get a partner who clearly loves the sound of their own voice, you can at least breathe a sigh of relief that there won't be any awkward silences. On the other hand, your challenge will be to credibly interject at some point and remind them that they're here for a reason – to learn about you.

A good way to do this, and to make the partner like you, is to be the person who can ask the interesting questions. Obviously you want to strike a good balance between not being too challenging and not being too kiss-ass.

What should I wear?

Business casual is usually the right way to go. The consultants will be wearing their 'work clothes' – it is very rare for them to change into casual clothes even in the evening. If in doubt, wear a suit – if you turn up and everyone has gone casual, you can quickly take off your coat and tie and roll up your sleeves. Similarly for women, if you err in one direction, err on formal that can be adapted easily.

Is there an etiquette around what to order?
Try not to stand out by ordering something massively expensive if nobody else is. Otherwise go for it.

More importantly, if the consultants are going straight for a main course, don't be the one who orders an appetizer. Perhaps they want to keep the dinner short. Same with dessert – go with the flow, don't stand out.

You won't usually have to guess about whether alcohol is appropriate. If this is a marketing event for them they'll usually ensure the wine is flowing freely (if you want to partake). But if nobody has ordered any drinks yet, perhaps you want to hang back until one of the consultants has set the tone.

With alcohol, be aware of what you are drinking. Be aware of how you behave after a couple of glasses of wine. Being relaxed and friendly is great – but you don't want to be the person at the table who suddenly appears to have had too much to drink.

Finally – I know I've said it already, but if you want to be remembered – send a thank you note!!

How should I make the best use of a one-on-one meeting ?
One of the events that you might come across is the opportunity to get some time to sit down one on one with a consultant. This may be at your school, either via an open sign-up or via invite, or perhaps it will be an offer to visit the office and meet the consultant.

Clearly this is a step up from the circle of death!

When I was a student going through recruiting I'm afraid to say I didn't ever sign up for such opportunities because I couldn't think of what to talk about. After all, surely the only real question is 'can I have a job?'!

Now I've been on the other side of the desk, as a consultant, and also as a career adviser who talks to many consultants about how they think such meetings can go well (and not so well) I have a more encouraging view. However, there are still pitfalls.

On the plus side – individual conversations are clearly a much better way for the consultant to get to know you, away from the scrum of the open cocktail event. It's also a chance for you (if you want) to ask some more detailed questions.

Getting to know you is in fact the main goal of the consultant, rather than selling the company to you. And yes, getting to know you *does* involve evaluation, so don't be fooled by any talk you might hear of such meetings being non-evaluative. Remember, you are always gaining or losing share.

So how is the consultant evaluating you?

This depends on the person, but there is probably some mix of conscious and unconscious evaluation. The conscious evaluation may involve looking out for evidence from you that you possess the skills that make a good consultant. These might include some basics, like do you come across as a polished professional, do you seem intelligent, are you eager to learn, are you enjoying Business School etc. The more advanced stuff might include do you think in a structured way? Do you have useful industry expertise? Are you able to put the consultant at ease and 'interview' them in a relaxed yet professional manner? The unconscious evaluation is more simple – do you 'feel ' like a consultant?

We'll talk more about this when we look at interviews, but for now think of it this way – since the consultant started work at her company, she has been exposed to a lot of people who are actually quite similar to each other. Beyond the fact that they start out similar, they then become even closer by learning to communicate, work, and even think in a similar way. You may think that I'm only referring to McKinsey, which as a firm has developed something of a reputation for turning people into 'clones', but this is a natural reaction to joining any group or culture. I've seen it at non-consulting companies just as often.

So the consultant sitting across from you in the meeting is actually weighing you up against the people she knows are already successful consultants. If you closely match a lot of the attributes, she will start to think that you too would 'fit in'. She may even think to herself – "this guy is just like my friend Tom who I worked with last month."

Surely this is about who you are, and can't really be 'gamed' or 'improved'?

I'd disagree, to a point.

Of course, you are not going to completely modify your personality. Why would you want to? Imagine if you completely put on a fake personality, and that fake person got all the way through recruiting. You'd end up surrounded by people who chose you because of a fake, and you'd have to carry on being that person. Deep down you'd know you didn't fit in, and that would probably end up showing. Don't be that person. Life's too short.

What you can do is to take the parts of your personality that you believe are already close to, or identical to, the type of person they're looking for, and either just plain make sure they notice those parts, or even accentuate them.

For instance: Consultants are invariably good at breaking down an issue into its component parts. You'll often hear them say "it sounds like there are three main points here..." or "I can see two main angles here, on the one hand there's X, on the other hand there's Y." You may have noticed I do a lot of this in the way I've written this book.

So if you too find yourself often communicating like this, make sure it comes across in the meeting.

Another example. Consultants are often excited about learning new stuff. You have to be, to choose a job where every few weeks or months you're thrown into a new problem, often in a new industry.

So if you are enjoying the fact that your MBA is exposing you to exciting new learning opportunities, perhaps you should emphasize that fact. Don't take it for granted. A lot of your classmates will come into the room, slump into the chair, and complain about how busy they are. That's not the kind of person a consultant is going to get excited about hiring!

A final example. As a consultant you have to be good at running meetings. This often involves taking what to an outsider can seem like a fairly transactional tone at the start, saying things like "We have 30 minutes, and here's what I want to get out of that time." I'd love it if someone came into my office and said that. I'd know that they'd given thought to how they can make this useful. If they gave me an objective that I thought was unreasonable, it would give me a chance to discuss that objective, and all through the meeting I'd have a sense of how well I was delivering on their goal.

Which leads us onto what not to do. Here are some things I've seen myself, and some that I've heard from recruiters:

- Don't interrogate the consultant. It's very off-putting and not at all fun if someone walks in to a room, sits down, and peppers you with incessant questions. That's not a conversation, it's an interrogation.
- Don't feel that you have to take up every minute of your allotted time. If the conversation is going really well, then of course you may end up using every last second allotted to you. But if you have had your questions answered after fifteen minutes, and you were booked in for half an hour, don't be

afraid to say so. It's always clear when someone starts to make up 'filler' questions, and can really sap the energy from what would otherwise have been a good conversation.

- Don't ask questions that they can't answer. Sounds obvious, but you'd be amazed at how many people used to ask me, when I worked at McKinsey, how I'd compare McKinsey to another company, let's say Bain. I can't answer that question simply because I don't have enough information, unless I previously worked at Bain. Equally, don't assume I know everything about my own company. When I worked in the London office, if you'd come in and started asking me about the Dallas office, I wouldn't be able to tell you a whole lot. Which is a shame, because I'd have had a lot to tell you about London that someone from Texas wouldn't be able to tell you. So make sure you are asking the right person the right question.

Final piece of advice – send a thank you note afterwards! (are you noticing a theme yet around thank you notes?!)

How should I reach out to alumni?

Your school may have a specific policy on this, but let's assume that you are given more or less open access to your alumni network – after all, that's a big reason you chose your school.

Many students come to me and say something along these lines - "I've heard I need to network with company X, and I've made a list of the alumni we have there – now what do I do?"

Many of these students have the feeling that they need to 'check off' each alum by having some kind of networking interaction. I think they have the image of building up points, one point for each alum that they have 'bagged'.

When I ask them what they want to talk to the alum about, they admit that they don't really have any reason to call or email, they just want to 'have had the contact'.

Imagine yourself in a few years' time. You are at your target company. You are very busy, to the point that you don't really have any free time that isn't taken up by sleep. You get an email from a student at your old business school, asking if you have 20 minutes to talk. You say "sure, I'd be glad to help out, because alumni helped me when I was in your position." Also you know that your company encourages its staff to get involved with recruiting.

The designated time for the call arrives, and you manage to get out of your team meeting, or perhaps you step out of a team dinner, or you manage to get phone reception while you are on the train home.

Thirty seconds into the call, you realize that the person on the phone has no real reason to call you. They are asking incredibly generic questions such as "so, what's it like working for company x?" You don't want to be rude, so you stick it out for the allotted 20 minutes.

Would you consider that a successful interaction for the student? Have they gained or lost share? I'd suggest that at best they have done nothing, because you'll probably forget about them. At worst, they annoyed you so actively that you'll make a note of their name to pass on the message to the recruiting team that this person called you but didn't have a plan for the conversation.

So let's rewind and see if we can come up with a version where the student 'gains share'.

Take a second.

What would that look like?

What would make you think that this was someone who had a genuine reason to call you?

I'm not going to give you a script here, because I don't want a thousand people next year calling alumni with exactly the same question!

But think about some of the things we've discussed in recent pages.

Try to find a personal connection – why did you choose this alum? Is it because they have a similar background to you? Perhaps it's just because they're the only recent alum from your school in the particular office you're most interested in. Perhaps you heard from a classmate that this alum is very friendly. Perhaps your career office recommended this alum as someone who has identified herself as happy to talk to students.

Let them know of the connection.

What do you want to get out of the discussion? Let them know up front. A general one might be that you are trying to build up an understanding of what day to day life is like, so you are asking a number of alumni to tell you about their best and worst day on the job. Perhaps you actually want advice on how someone from your background, industry or country could best position themselves – in that case why not let the alum know that you have called specifically to ask their advice (people like being asked to give advice). Perhaps you are asking for an onward lead. You might be very focused on the energy practice and have found that so far your school doesn't have any alumni in that practice, so you are calling the alum to ask their advice on anyone in energy you could speak with, and how to approach that person.

To conclude:

- Have an objective for the call.
- Let the alum know your objective.

- Ideally pick someone with a logical connection to you.
- If you can't think of a reason for the call, don't ask for the call!

Should you send a reminder email if your first one is not answered?

This is what happened to me a few times: I'd get an email from someone from my old business school. I'd mean to respond, but it wouldn't be a priority because at that moment I'd have a number of other urgent things. Then it would slip from my mind.

If the student ever sent me a second email, politely asking me if I'd had a chance to see their first email, and checking to see if I'd be able to give them even just 10 minutes, I'd invariably reply. I'd feel bad that I hadn't replied the first time. I'd be glad they'd given me a prod. If I was genuinely too busy I'd let them know, but I'd never hold it against them for asking for the time.

That's just me, but I imagine that most people are happy to help, if and when they have time.

If your second email goes unanswered, that's probably a sign that the person is either too busy or isn't interested. Time for you to move on to someone else.

How should I think about the recruiter compared to the consultants?

Bearing in mind everything we've covered so far, it should be clear that every interaction you have with every member of the consulting company is an opportunity for you to gain or lose share.

In addition to the consultants that you meet, there will often be a member of the HR staff who is the 'recruiter'. Perhaps that person's full time job is to manage recruiting at your school.

If it's still not clear whether you should consider the recruiter a key person, let's recap what they do:

- They manage your file
- They manage your application
- They decide who will interview you
- They sit in on the meeting where your hiring decision is made

Call me crazy, but I'd want that person to think favorably of me!

Many people forget this. There are a number of events where the recruiter will also be present but will not be center stage – perhaps the open reception after a briefing, perhaps a dinner, perhaps a wine tasting, perhaps the ten minutes outside the interview room before you get interviewed. Many people will ignore the recruiter and leave him or her standing there like a piece of unwanted furniture. Don't be that person! Be the one who engages the recruiter in conversation – show interest in them, show empathy for the fact that the big event you are attending was probably a major piece of work for them to organize.

Summary of networking

We've covered a lot of ground in this section, but there are some definite themes that keep coming back:

- Successful networking can be a useful part of getting onto a company's closed list
- Networking is not about selling – it is simply giving the company the chance to get to know you and to decide for itself if you look like an interesting candidate
- There are many opportunities for you to allow the company to gather information about you
- Remember that every interaction with the company is a chance not only for you to 'gain share', but also to 'lose share'

- The single most important element of networking is the thank-you email
- Don't ask people for their time unless you have a reason for the conversation
- Be nice to everyone, including the recruiter

The job application

So you've learnt about the job and decided which companies you'll apply for. Now there's only one thing standing between you and the interview – actually applying and being chosen!

You may be lucky enough to be at a school where your target company is able to interview everyone who wants to apply. In that case, this chapter won't apply to you. For the majority of cases, though, there will be a selection process.

In terms of that process, you want to make sure you know the answers to the following questions:

For each opportunity you want to apply to:

- When is the application deadline?
- How will you submit your application?
- What materials and information does the company require?

If I were you, I'd create some kind of spreadsheet that listed out the above information. As we all know, being a student at B school keeps you kind of busy. The last thing you want to happen is to find out that you missed out on your dream job because you weren't aware of the deadline, or because when you finally came to make your application you found out that the company required information you didn't have at your fingertips.

When is the application deadline?

Find out this date and make sure you also make a note of the time! At Tuck many of our internal deadlines are midday. This is not immediately intuitive (you may think that you have until midnight for instance).

For any kind of job posting, the deadline (and time if relevant) will be given. Perhaps the posting will be on your school's internal system. Perhaps it will be on the company website.

How will you submit your application?
There are two main options:

1. The company itself will have a website where you make your application
2. Your school will have an internal process (perhaps a website or a folder on a shared drive)

Confusingly, you may need to do both.

Make sure you are aware of the submission procedure, and if it is a company website, go and check it out as soon as possible. Often you will be able to log in and start your application. This will give you a good idea of what the application will involve.

What materials and information will the company require?
Remember business school or college applications? Remember how many arcane pieces of information and paperwork they asked for?

- Some companies may ask for many of the same pieces of information again.
- Some may ask for new information.
- Some may only require a resume.

Make sure you are aware of what your target company requires – and make sure you give yourself enough time to gather the information.

Here are some questions I frequently get on application materials

Will they ask for my GMAT score?
- Probably. Most companies do. Whatever you think of it, the GMAT is at least a standardized test that almost all MBA students took. If I were running recruiting at a consulting company, I'd ask for it. If you didn't take the GMAT, you will probably be able to use the GRE instead.

What is a good GMAT score?

- The answer to this is the same as when you were applying to B school.

Should I retake my GMAT if I didn't get a good score?

- There's no perfect answer for this. If you are reading this before you have arrived at B school, AND you have a lot of spare time, AND you believe that your current GMAT score does not accurately reflect your true ability, what have you got to lose?

Will they ask for my MBA grades (so far)?

- Probably. You've spent the last few months, or perhaps more than a year, studying the kinds of things that you need to be good at in order to be a consultant. Now you have grades that to some extent give an unbiased view on how good you are and/or how hard you have worked. If I owned a consulting company and I knew you'd just taken a class on Excel modeling, I'd ask how you did in that class.

My school has a non-disclosure policy for grades. What if the company asks for grades?

- Clearly you will want to follow the policy of your school. If you are not allowed to disclose grades then you shouldn't
- If you are allowed to, then you should. Do you want to work at that company or not?

The position requires Permanent Work Authorization (PWA). I am not a US citizen, but I know that as an MBA student I am allowed to work in the US for the summer and then for a year after my MBA.

- Permanent Work Authorization generally means that you are a citizen or a Permanent Resident (green card holder)
- If the application requires evidence of work authorization, be honest about your visa status. Chances are that the company knows the difference between CPT and H-1B.

- Every year, I see talented non-residents get jobs that were originally specified as requiring PWA. These happen on a case by case basis where the student is particularly well qualified for the role (usually because of prior work experience). In these cases, there will be conversations that happen outside of (and before) the paperwork of the application process being filed.
- For any more discussion of work authorization, you should speak with your career services. This is a complex issue and the rules change.

The resume
Your resume is a reflection of your work experience

This sounds obvious, so why did I state it?

I think many applicants get into the mindset that the resume writing process is a chance for everyone to start with the same blank-sheet, and for the 'best-written' resume to win the day.

This is not the case

This isn't an essay writing contest, or an exam, where everyone starts with zero points, and then what you choose to put on the page starts giving you points until the person with the best written document gets the most points.

Put another way. The content of your resume can flex a certain percentage, but it will always be grounded by the facts of your life.

If there is someone out there who represented their country in the Olympics, then climbed Mount Everest, and then started Facebook, whilst at the same time founding a nationwide non-profit that cured a major disease – that person's resume is going to 'beat' yours, no matter how badly they screw up the bullet points, and no matter how many hours you spend polishing yours.

If someone else out there is applying for a consulting job but has no work experience (for an MBA level job), a poor GMAT score, no extra-curricular activities and nothing else to add, then it really doesn't matter how beautifully they craft the sentence that describes their contribution to the consulting club. Whether they 'spearheaded' the case marathon, or 'led', 'managed', 'initiated', or 'drove results' will not move their resume to the top of the pile.

These are two extremes, but bear them in mind.

The takeaways for this are:

- Everyone's resume is different
- Content will win over style
- Once you are happy that your resume accurately reflects the content you believe consulting companies are looking for, you should spend an hour or so polishing the style and checking for errors, then you should consider yourself done

So what content are they looking for?

Type of work and the way you did it

Think back over the presentations and networking events. What have you learnt about <u>the type of work that consultants do, and the way they do it?</u>

- They work in teams
- They counsel clients
- They gather information and analyze it
- They present difficult information in a way that is easy to digest

Look back through your own experience, and emphasize the above elements when you describe the things you have done.

Type of person you are

Again, think back over the presentations, the office visits, the networking you have done. What have you heard about the personality traits and competencies they look for? What have you observed from the people you've met?

Here's my starter list (you could probably add some more)

- Clever
- Hard-working
- Intellectually curious
- Entrepreneurial
- Creative
- Fun to be around

So how can your resume reflect the above?

Here are some thoughts. Not all will apply, and this is not exhaustive.

- If you are clever and hardworking you probably got a good GMAT score. If so, include that.
- If you worked in a company that valued the above qualities, perhaps you were promoted, or recognized with some kind of award, or got a good result in your performance evaluation. If so, talk about that.
- If you have the above qualities, perhaps you have gone to good schools, and received scholarships aimed at attracting such people.
- If you are entrepreneurial, perhaps you have founded, or started something. It doesn't have to be a company. Perhaps you started an initiative within an organization, or improved the way something happened.
- If you are intellectually curious and creative, perhaps you have written something that was published? Perhaps you worked on something groundbreaking?
- If you are fun to be around, perhaps you have interesting personal activities? Perhaps you can even allow your personality to come through in the way you describe those activities?

Type of language to use - Look to the future, not the past
A key here is to use the language of the job you are applying for, not of your past. This is particularly true if you came from an industry where technical jargon was commonplace. It may be impressive in your old firm that you increased POS of LM NMEs, or used your SQL knowledge to rationalize the legacy server estate, but you run a significant risk that the recruiter at your dream consulting job does not understand what you are saying. You should assume that the reader does not have any industry or function specific expertise, and explain accordingly.

What's the 'so what'?
This is a slightly annoying phrase that consultants use (talking about insider jargon!). What it means is – why are you telling me this?

Here's an example.

A student might write a bullet that says

'Led team to re-design workflow in advance of roll-out of new device.'

There are several ways you could make this better.

Quantifiable result: Did your re-designed workflow result in 10% faster or cheaper results? Were you recognized by the CEO for your performance? Did you get a bonus or promotion?

Difficulty of task: Did you have to assemble a team across different functions? Were you the most senior person or did you have to lead via influence? Were you up against a significant deadline? Were you out of your depth in any way?

Accuracy and completeness
I'll include this not because I think you are stupid, but because I know you are busy and probably stressed:

Check your resume for mistakes
- A good way to proof a document is to print it out and go through it line by line.

- An even better way is to have someone else proof it for you.

Check it contains everything it should do (including phone number, address, etc.)
- Check that the phone number you have listed actually works, and that there is voicemail set up.

The cover letter

Similar to the resume, a lot of students tend to approach the letter with the thought that everyone starts with an equal chance of being selected for interview, and that the quality of the letter alone is what will get them on the closed list.

In reality, for consulting the cover letter is the least important element when compared to the resume and the networking interactions you have had.

Over the past couple of years, I've asked recruiters to weight the above factors, with a question along the lines of:

How important, out of a total of 100%, are resume, cover letter and networking to a student's chance of getting an interview.

The average response is:

Resume – 40 to 50%

Networking interactions – 40 to 50%

Cover letter – About 10%

Worryingly, the most common case that recruiters cite of a cover letter changing a student's chance of getting an interview is that a mistake on the letter will reduce that chance (or perhaps even instantly destroy it).

What makes a good cover letter?

There are a number of things that a cover letter can usefully do:

Shows that you can write a professional, concise, error free document

This is not a trivial matter. As a consultant, a key part of your job will be producing documents that get complex issues across in a simple manner. Above all, you will require a focus on detail and accuracy. It is unacceptable to have a mistake in a client presentation, and it is similarly unacceptable to have a mistake in your cover letter.

Answers any questions that your resume may raise

When I read through your resume, does it leave me with any questions or concerns? Hopefully not, but sometimes there's something that stands out. Often this is a gap in employment, or a transition from one job to another that does not look intuitive.

Is there a very big leap between your background and the job you are applying for? This is less critical than people think, as consulting companies are very used to hiring people with non-consulting backgrounds, but if your whole resume looks like it was leading you one way and now you are taking a major left turn, perhaps you want to talk about that.

Gives a sense of how passionate you are for the company

This is not always possible. Probably you are applying to 10 companies, all of which are similar, and all of which would be pretty good to work for. Sometimes, however, I'll read a letter that makes it abundantly clear that the applicant is REALLY excited about the specific company. Usually the interest in the company started before business school, and the 'relationship' is more than a couple of networking interactions. It's actually easier with product companies (for instance if you are applying to Microsoft you can talk about all of their products that you have been using since birth). Sometimes with consulting you may have worked alongside that company before, or have a friend or relative who has worked there. Or perhaps you have noticed that the company writes a lot of material that your former industry relies on. You won't really be able to manufacture this, but if it is the case, you should let the company know.

Gives a sense of your personality
I do see some letters that give me a genuine feel for the personality of the writer. Mostly this is a good thing. If you feel there are parts of your personality that are attractive to a recruiter (perhaps your approachability, your sense of humor, your self-confident ability to mix professionalism with fun, your soft skills, your emotional intelligence), then why not try to get that across?

The upside of this is that hopefully your letter will stand out. After all, in a batch of 200 cover letters to Bain, every letter will be about Bain. Only one will be about you.

The potential downside is that you misjudge your reader, or don't execute as skillfully as you'd thought, and the tone comes across wrong.

So, to summarize:

- Be organized, and get started early – companies may ask for a lot of information and you don't want to miss the deadline.
- Your resume should be written in the language of the job you are applying for, with little or no technical or industry specific jargon.
- If you are spending all weekend on one letter you are probably over-thinking it.
- Good content and style can sometimes help your candidacy.
- Mistakes will ALWAYS negatively affect your candidacy.

Succeeding in interviews

Consulting interviews usually consist of a number of components, spread out across a number of rounds of interview.

Each round would usually entail you being interviewed by more than one person.

So a representative process might be something like this:

- First round – two interviews, each one hour long. On campus.
- Second (decision round) – three interviews, each one hour long. At the office.

Each interview will be made up of one or more of the following common elements:

- **Case interview**
  The case interview is a standard part of consulting recruiting. Usually it is a one-on-one discussion, although some firms like to put people in groups and let them collaborate.

- **Fit interview**
  More like a 'regular' job interview, this is where they seek to get an understanding of you, your history, your strengths and weaknesses etc.

- **Presentation**
  Since presenting is such a core part of consulting, many firms build some kind of presentation into their interview. You may be asked to prepare something in advance, or you may be given a question on the day, then left alone for a period to prepare your presentation.

Case interviews

There are many excellent books and resources on how to succeed in case interviews, so I'll try not to duplicate what they cover, but I would like to add what I've learnt over the last few years – first as a student going through the process, then as an interviewer at McKinsey, and most recently as a career counselor.

Here's what I propose to cover in this chapter, based on the most common discussions I have with students and recruiters. The points are roughly chronological in terms of when in the process they tend to arise.

- What is a case interview?
- Why do firms use case interviews?
- Which book/resource should I buy?
- Is it worth practicing with fellow students when neither of us knows what we're doing?
- Should I take advantage of mock cases with firm representatives?
- How can I give cases and give useful feedback?
- How many practice cases should I do?
- Isn't it all about intrinsics? Can I genuinely improve?
- What do they mean by structure?
- Why can't I just memorize a bunch of existing structures?
- How do I know whether I should lead the case or not?
- How can I improve my public math?
- How can I improve my creative thinking?
- What is an 'answer-first' summary?
- I've got the basics, but what are they *really* looking for?
- What is the difference between a first and second round interview?
- Why was the partner rude to me?

What is a case interview?

A case interview is a type of interview that uses a business problem to provide the content that you and the interviewer will discuss.

It could be a hypothetical situation, or a situation the interviewer has faced in her consulting work.

Usually it does not require prior knowledge (the interviewer should give you all the information you need – sometimes verbally and sometimes via printed exhibits).

Very often you will use notepaper to keep track of your thoughts, and often to communicate with the interviewer (for instance to show them a list or organized set of things you want to cover).

Often there will be some way of testing your math skills – either a written calculation you will have to do or a piece of mental arithmetic that you need to perform.

Often there will be a chance for you to demonstrate your business sense and ability to think creatively.

There are some short cases and some long ones, but the average is probably 20 minutes to half an hour.

Sometimes there is a 'right' answer that you are meant to arrive at, and other times it is more ambiguous – either way it is the way you conduct the conversation that is being tested, not just the conclusion.

Why do firms use case interviews?

The problem with traditional job interviews is that they very often come down to a matter of 'do I like this person'. It is very difficult to get a sense of how the person will actually perform on the job. That's why for many jobs that involve practical skills, you would get the person to demonstrate their ability to perform that skill.

Think of an actor going to a 'job interview' for a part in a play. It would be ridiculous for the casting director to simply ask the actor to talk about his resume, his part in leading a team, and his opinion on where he wants to be in five years. Clearly, the actor will be asked to show how good he is at acting.

Similarly, If you were screening young soccer players, you might get them to run some drills – you'd want to see how fast they can sprint, how well they can control the ball, how they interact with the rest of the team, etc.

Consulting is not as obvious a practical skill as acting or playing soccer, but it is still the application of a set of intellectual and social skills. The case interview is designed as a simulation that allows the interviewer to get a fairly close understanding of how you perform when thinking about a new problem.

I've given a lot of case interviews. At first I wasn't sure I'd be able to give a correctly calibrated opinion on how somebody performed, and it probably took me a while to get to the point where I had a good sense of 'bad', 'average' and 'good' performance. But now I've done enough that I really do believe the interviews let me see quite a lot about your thought processes, the way you interact, and the way you handle pressure. Having also been a consultant for quite a while, both as an entry level consultant and also as a manager, I also have a fairly strong belief that the skills I'm testing for in the interview are those skills I'd be looking for in my team during a consulting engagement. To conclude - I do believe that the interview is a pretty good 'audition' for the job.

Which book/resource should I buy?
Type 'case interview' into Google or Amazon and you'll find a number of resources standing by to help you, including one of my books.

Obviously, having written a book, 'Case Interviews For Beginners', I recommend you start there! Of course I'm biased, but I believe it's a good starting point.

After that, I don't have a strong opinion on which resource is best.

If you like to be given a roadmap, with elements to memorize in case you blank, then Marc Cosentino's book may be for you – Marc has a number of classic elements that you can memorize, and these are very useful to get you out of trouble, as long as you then filter them through your own experience and language (e.g., don't just regurgitate).

If you want a solid set of practice cases, with exhibits and guides for the case-giver, then David Ohrvall's book may be for you, along with the videos on his website.

One thing I would say is perhaps you should value diversity. If everyone in your class has bought the same book, there will be a risk that when a company comes to campus to interview, every student will betray the fact that they're all working off the same page. Or perhaps you should read a few of the books to ensure that you don't get all of your ideas from one place.

Is it worth practicing with fellow students when neither of us knows what we're doing?

So let's assume you bought a book, have familiarized yourself with the basic concept, and now want to start getting some actual practice under your belt.

When I was a student at Tuck, the way it worked was that the consulting club would organize a few days when all the students who were seeking to learn case interviews could get together and practice. In addition, we would each seek each other out (usually starting with friends and people who we felt would give good practice). Once we felt we had the basics, we would seek out people with more experience, often second year students who'd done an internship in consulting, or classmates who'd been consultants before school.

The above approach works pretty well (it worked for me).

Low quality, high volume

The obvious downside is that when two beginners get together to do a practice case, the quality of the case from either point of view is quite low. It's a bit like asking someone who is very out of shape to be your fitness training partner. As with this analogy, it's better than nothing, and perhaps when you are starting out there is something to be said for doing low impact work. I actually think that for the bulk of your practice, there's nothing wrong with doing these 'low quality' practice sessions if the flipside is that you can get in a high volume. Because with case practice volume is one of your goals.

Stepping it up a notch

There should come a time when you feel that practicing with friends isn't stretching you enough. To continue with the fitness training analogy, you've started to build up your muscles and stamina, and now you're looking for a training partner who can push you further.

- At this point you really want someone who can take you out of your comfort zone. The easiest way to do this is to find another person in your class who is learning cases, but is someone you don't know. Doing cases with your friend can get cozy and easy, so doing them with strangers brings back that adrenaline.
- In addition to getting out of your comfort zone, you really want to find people who are masters of case interviews. The most obvious next step at a two year Business School is a second year student who got the job last year. These are definitely higher quality interviewers than your friends, although you should bear in mind that these people may not be 100% sure what it was about their performance that got them the job. Hopefully, though, they are intuitive enough to have a good sense, and a good enough teacher that they can give you useful feedback.

Seek out people who know what they are doing, but are 'safe'

- The last level of 'safe' practice is to find people who have been trained how to give case interviews, and who have done it in an evaluative setting, but are not currently employed by your target firm. If you are at Tuck, this would be me. If you are not, there may be someone in career services with these criteria, or perhaps a professor or other staff member who is a former consultant. In addition, you may have friends or former colleagues in this category. Finally, there are a number of excellent online services such as Evisors where you can pay to do practice interviews with such people.

Should I take advantage of mock cases with firm representatives?

Finally, we leave behind the safe harbor of non-evaluative practice and get to the point where you take advantage of firms' offers of practice interviews. At Tuck, before the real interviews get started, many firms send up their consultants (often recent graduates), to give students the opportunity to do a case.

These interviews are a great way to get 'live-fire' practice. You really will get the adrenaline rush, the uncomfortable sense that you are about to say something really stupid, the terrifying feeling that suddenly the ability to do simple math has deserted you. This kind of practice can be really powerful, because if you went from cozy interviews with friends straight into the real interview, you might be in for a shock.

But be careful! Think about where in the process you are. If the firm has not yet selected its interview candidates, you can be sure that your performance in a practice will feed into that selection decision. The best way to try to manage this is to be sure that you tell your interviewer where you feel you are in the journey from beginner to interview-ready. If you have only done one or two practices, tell them that.

If the interview list has been selected, you are still being evaluated. Here there is a potential upside. Let's say you do a practice case with a firm member, and you really ace it. If you then make a trivial mistake in the real interview, there is a chance that your performance in the practice case may get discussed.

How can I give cases and give useful feedback?

If someone asks you to give them a case, there are a number of fairly simple things you can do to dramatically increase the value that you bring to the practice. Giving a case is a skill in itself, so don't just assume that you can glance through a question, print out the exhibits, and then give a useful practice case. Take some time to think about the case you are about to give, with emphasis on the following elements:

Understand and have mastery of the case you are giving.

Giving a case is difficult. The most difficult is when an interviewee comes to you and says 'can we use X case – I've brought it with me'. At that point you have to go through it blind – getting the information at the same time as the interviewee. Very often these kinds of cases turn into a strange kind of treasure hunt. You know that you have an exhibit about sales data to hand over, and the interviewee knows you have it, and you are simply waiting for them to ask the right question. I can tell when students come to me for case practice if they have had a lot of these experiences. Essentially their method of being interviewed has ended up as them asking a lot of questions that sound a lot like 'do we have data for X?', 'How about data for Y?', 'OK, do we have data for Z'?

It's a lot easier to give a satisfying case interview if you have some mastery of the content. The best way to do this is to make up your own case. Think of an industry you are familiar with, and then think of a common issue in that industry. Or take one of the common case questions (a company is thinking of expanding into X market, two companies are considering a merger, company X is considering launching Y new product) and make up a version in your industry. If you want data, you could either make some up, or you could look through case books for a similar case and take that data. You should really try this, because I know you're thinking it sounds too difficult, but it's really not, and the case you give will be a lot more satisfying.

If you can't, or don't, do the above, then the next best thing is to find a case in a book and repeatedly give that case. You will start to see variations in the performances, styles, etc. of the people you give it to. It helps if you have found a reasonably obscure case so that you can be sure that nobody else is using it. Or, if you are with a group or club, why not start out the 'season' by each person taking a case from a book – that way you can be sure that your one won't be used by everyone else.

Useful tips through the case (for an interviewer)

Here are some things that work well for me, and that will hopefully make you sound more like a 'real' case interviewer. You don't need to do all of these things all of the time, but they are useful tools to have on hand.

Some of them are helpful, in that they allow the person to give more explanation, and get them used to talking through their thought process. Others are designed to stress the interviewee, partly to see how they react to stress, and in this situation partly to give them practice at being stressed in a case interview.

- **Ask for more.**

  When they have described the main chunks of their structure, ask if there's anything they're missing. Watch how they react to that. Even if you are absolutely certain they have got everything, push them for more.

- **Challenge them.**

  When they assert or assume something (for instance, they may assert that they want to look at the overall market, or they may make an assumption about the attractiveness of a certain business) challenge that. Ask why they assume that. Ask why they think that looking at the market is useful?

- **Ask why they want information.**

If you are faced with the data request without rationale ("Do we have any information on competitors?") push your interviewee by asking them why they want that information, and what they intend to do with it.

- **Give them the silent treatment.**
  If they are looking to you for guidance, keep quiet.

- **Interrupt them**

  If they are happily talking away and you think they have covered their main point, interrupt them to ask a question, or perhaps just to say "Let's move on".

Design your criteria for feedback and keep track of performance through the case

When a real interviewer is giving you a case, they are grading you on a certain set of criteria. Each company will have slightly different criteria, but really they are all looking for the same concepts. I'll lay them out here and you can use these, or you can design your own wordings of the same concepts. Note that these are not word for word the criteria I was trained to use by McKinsey – I don't feel it would be right for me to give away that information, although you may get lucky and have some other member of that or any of your other target firms tell you the actual criteria (in which case, be sure you write that down and refer to it often!).

Ability to structure a plan to answer the question

Consulting is often about coming up with customized ways of dealing with unique problems. The interviewee needs to be able to listen to a new problem, probably something quite complex, in an industry they may never have thought about before, and then design a plan for how they will solve that. Very often this plan will be written out as an issue tree, or a set of topics.

This ability to bring structure to a question is not only to be tested at the start. If you have follow-up questions, or any secondary issues in the case, look out for how the interviewee is bringing structure to bear. Sometimes it may be as simple as saying 'well, there seem to be pros and cons to this, so let's start with the pros...'

Common sense, business acumen and creativity

Once they've laid out their structure, pay attention to the actual ideas they come up with. Are these ideas sensible? Do they cover a broad range, including pretty much everything you would have thought of yourself? Do they come up with interesting thoughts that nobody else has yet come up with? Do they use analogies, or refer to existing knowledge?

Ability to do the numbers

Your case should have some quantitative element to it. It may be a data table or graph you are asking them to interpret. It may be a market sizing question you set them. It may be a complex calculation you ask them to design and then work through. Whatever it is, you should look out for a couple of things:

- How comfortable do they seem? Do they shy away from the calculations or do they leap right in?
- Can they structure the calculation? If you have asked for a market sizing, or a complex calculation, do they get the logic right?
- Can they actually do the arithmetic? (Don't worry too much about how long they take) —do they get the right number? If they don't, do they pick up on their mistake?

Do they act in a professional manner, and 'feel' like a consultant?

> As they are going through the case, are they treating you like a colleague or a client (either is fine)? Or are they nervously focusing on their paper and failing to look you in the eye (not fine)? Do they sound hesitant, or do they sound confident? When they are thinking, do they look like they are panicking, or do they look like they are enjoying wrestling with this puzzle?

> Some overall questions you should ask yourself are – would I trust this person with a client? Would I want to spend time with this person? Would I want to work with them? Would I feel safe knowing that they were working on a difficult problem in a stressful situation?

> Think about the consultants you have met so far – does this person act like one of those? (probably reasonably confident, friendly, professional etc.)

Giving feedback

So now you have your criteria – hopefully as you gave your case, you took notes on how the interviewee performed in each of the above areas.

Before launching into giving feedback, I usually ask the interviewee how they think they did. Often they give a fairly accurate and comprehensive summary of their performance. They tend to err on being too negative on themselves. Let them talk until it is clear they have finished.

Be thoughtful about the feedback you give. Learning a new skill is difficult and the person is probably feeling fairly vulnerable. So be sure to tell them about everything they did well. And if they did really well, let them know.

If you are providing negative feedback, it can often be helpful to ask if that particular piece of feedback is something they have heard before.

Often the response will be "yes, everyone says that about me." In which case, that is a good starting point for some discussion on how to overcome that particular weakness.

For negative feedback, try to use specifics. It's not useful to say "I didn't really feel you did all that well on the math." It's a lot more useful for you to say, "when you laid out your approach to the market sizing, you were very hesitant, and if we look at the steps you laid out, you didn't provide a logical way of justifying how many gas stations you assumed per town." Keeping to specifics makes it about them, not about you.

If it turns out that you are the first person to have made this negative comment, perhaps you are either more perceptive or brave than others, or perhaps this performance was atypical, or perhaps you are just wrong.

How many practice cases should I do?
You should practice until you feel ready. Some people will feel ready after five or ten cases. Others will take upwards of 100.

What are some clues that you are ready?

- People you respect tell you that you are ready
- You genuinely believe that a case interview is a great way to demonstrate your potential as a consultant
- You find that doing a case is now not about the mechanics of drawing a structure and doing math, but is a great way to discuss an interesting business situation
- You feel confident that for any type of case question you could have an interesting conversation and probably arrive at the right answer
- You routinely nail the math portion of any case you do, and any math practice you are doing
- It's been a while since you had a disastrous practice case

- You have found a number of common structures (hopefully in your own language) that you are successfully using in many situations
- From having given a lot of cases, you have a good feel for the elements that make up a good performance
- When you give cases to your friends and classmates, you often feel that you could have done the case as well or perhaps even better than they did

Isn't it all about intrinsics? Can I genuinely improve?

A case interview done well can provide a good insight into the way you think, and your strength at thinking in a number of ways. **There are people who excel at these ways of thinking, and there are people who simply aren't wired that way.** Therefore there is probably a large chunk of the population who wouldn't succeed in a case interview no matter how much practice they got. *For this concept, let's use the analogy of a town full of people who all set out to become champion weight lifters.* Some of them are going to be naturals. Others are never going to make it, no matter how great their technique or how many hours of training they put in. This is not about ability, or quality, but about how you fit with the characteristics required by the job. In other words, if you are a wimpy guy like me, you are never going to be a champion weight-lifter, but I don't think that reflects on my quality as a human being.

If you are at Business School, then you likely have most of all of the skills required – consulting is very similar to Business School. The screening criteria that got you in to Business School are close to the criteria that consulting companies use. That is why consulting companies recruit at Business Schools. *This is more like a group of people who are regular members of a gym who decide to become weightlifters.*

A case interview is a highly artificial thing, and is not something that anybody was born good at. Therefore, even people who have the potential to succeed will not succeed without any training or practice. *A better analogy for this would be people who set out to be great golf players*. A golf swing is simply not a natural thing. You can't win at Augusta without putting in the hours of practice, no matter if you have the innate physique or not.

So, using the above logic:

- Most people at Business School could meet the bar in terms of intrinsic 'ability', although even within that set of people there will be a range.
- Everyone will need a certain amount of training and practice.
- Some people will find it relatively easy, and will not need a lot of practice. Many people will find it a struggle, but will get there with practice. Some people will lack the intrinsic fit with the ways of thinking required by the job and/or will not practice enough, and will not succeed.

If you want more input on this discussion, ask people who you respect who are now consultants about the way they approached case interviews. You will not meet many, if any, who say they simply turned up and did the interview without ever practicing. And you will hear a range of answers if you ask a lot of them how much practice they did.

What do they mean by structure?

This one really had me puzzled for a long time when I was a student learning about case interviews. People would invariably talk about using a structure, or a framework (terms which seem in this context to be fairly interchangeable) .

So, here's my input on this somewhat confused and messy subject:

First, let's start by describing the absence of structure... What does unstructured thought look like?

Let's use the example of me doing renovation work on my house. If you ask me what I've got to do I might tell you:

- Buy electrical boxes
- Strip wallpaper
- Buy light-fittings
- Research painting techniques
- Buy paint and paint-brushes
- Learn how to fit lights and electrical boxes
- Paint the walls
- Install the electrical fittings

This is clearly an unstructured list. It also fairly accurately reflects the way my brain might work, particularly when I'm stressed, or when things seem very complicated.

If you were my friend, and I described the above list of activities to you, you might be able to help me by adding some structure to it. You could do it in a number of ways.

By area of work

- Electrical
  - Learn how to fit lights and electrical boxes
  - Buy electrical boxes
  - Buy light-fittings
  - Install the electrical fittings

- Painting
  - Research painting techniques
  - Strip wallpaper
  - Buy paint and paint-brushes
  - Paint the walls

Or by phase of work

- Planning and research
  - Research painting techniques
  - Learn how to fit lights and electrical boxes

- Buying
  - Buy electrical boxes
  - Buy light-fittings
  - Buy paint and paint-brushes

- Doing
  - Strip wallpaper
  - Paint the walls
  - Install the electrical fittings

There are a number of advantages such structuring:

- It makes the whole problem seem manageable
- It's easy to communicate
- It helps me to check if there are any gaps

I saw such structuring work very effectively when I was working as a consultant. All of the above advantages are very powerful when you are working with important problems and stressed clients.

Manageable

It sounds simple, but it can be very useful if you can talk with a client for half an hour about all of their problems, and then say to them "OK, so what I heard you say is that you have three main tasks ahead, you need to plan your work, then you need to go on a shopping trip, then you need to roll up your sleeves and do the work." The response I often got was "Yes, you understand my situation well, and now that you've described it like that it seems achievable."

Easy to communicate

Let's say I'm the project manager of the house renovation, and I have a lot of people coming along to help out. Every time someone arrives I need to tell them what's going on and assign them a task. If I only the have the first list, I'll tell them everything that's on my mind and they won't remember it. On the other hand, if I tell them "OK, we've got to do some research, go shopping, then start work", they'll understand immediately. I could even make up a planner that said – Monday – do research ; Tuesday – go shopping; Wed onward – do work...

Gap checking

This is pretty useful. With my initial list, there was no way of telling if I'd got everything. Now I can look at the headings and ask myself – Will my house be done once I've painted and done the electrical work? Is there anything else? Oh yes, what about the flooring!

Equally, within a category, I can quickly scan each section. If I push myself to come up with more ideas, I'll certainly think of some. Better now than halfway through the project when I realize that I should have added 'buy screwdriver' to the electrical section.

At the start of a case, when the interviewer gives you a question, they're often playing the role of the confused client, to whom the problem seems very difficult and unmanageable. What they're looking for is a person who can pretty quickly assimilate that new problem, and come up with a manageable, easy to communicate plan that incidentally allows for gap checking.

For example:

Initial question:

The client is a US fast food chain that is looking to expand into India. Should they go ahead?

What goes through your head in the next ten seconds probably approximates the various issues that the client is aware of: issues that make this a difficult decision. Those issues might include:

- There are a lot of people in India – seems like it would be great if we could tap into that market!
- Does anyone at the client have experience in India?
- Do Indians like American fast food?
- Aren't a lot of Indians vegetarian?
- How do they run the operation in the US – is it a franchise model?
- Would you use the same décor and color scheme in India?
- What kinds of food retailers would you be competing against?
- Are there any laws stopping US companies from setting up food operations in India?
- Do our US management team have time to think about this?
- Who would run this new Indian division?

In real life, as a consultant, you may have had a meeting with a client who is tasked with answering this question – it may be a big question the whole company is focused on or it may be something that has come up along the way. The client may, over the course of an hour, mention all of the above thoughts, and ask for your help.

Some of the most effective consultants I've worked with have really honed the skill of listening to a 'brain dump' like the one above and then summarizing by saying something like:

"Ok, so from what we've discussed, it sounds like there are three major questions we need to answer: First, is there a demand in India for our kind of restaurant? Second, are there already competitors in this space? Third, does our company have the ability to launch this expansion? If we can answer all of those, then we'll be in a good position to make a decision on whether this is a good move. Have I got that right, or is there anything we've missed?"

To use our criteria from above, this is useful for the client because it suddenly makes the task ahead seem **manageable**, the work ahead is now **easy to communicate**, both within the client organization and to our fellow consultants who may be working with us, and laying out the main categories makes it easy to **check for gaps**. For instance, comparing the consultant's summary above with the clients list of questions might reveal a gap in terms of regulations or laws that might stop us. So the client might respond to the consultant that there is probably a fourth category and that could be incorporated into the work.

The reason I'm sharing this is because I want you to understand that coming up with a structure to answer a question is not an abstract test. It is a skill that consultants use that has real, practical value.

So, how do you show that you have this skill in the interview?

A good answer, then, to the above interview questions might go something like:

"OK, so if our client wants to understand if they should launch into India, I think I'd like to investigate the following issues:

First, is there a market for our client's product in India. I'm curious about this because I suspect that Indians and Americans have very different tastes, and clearly if there's no demand from the consumers then it wouldn't be a sensible move.

Secondly, if there is a market, is there anyone already in that space? Perhaps one of our major competitors might already be there, or perhaps there are a lot of local operators who have restaurants that we would be competing against. If we're going to plan a launch into this market, I'd want a clear understanding of the competitors so we could first of all decide if there's a chance we could win, and secondly so we could form our tactics accordingly.

Thirdly, I'd want to know if our client has the capabilities to make such an expansion. That might include things like the bandwidth of the senior management team, it would also include people who know the local market, or who have experience in entering new countries. Some of these capabilities could probably be acquired if we don't have them. Also in terms of capability I'd want to look at the logistics of how we could do this – would we franchise? Would we ship the ingredients from a central supply or would we source them locally?

Finally, I'd want to check that there aren't trade restrictions or laws stopping us from making this move. I don't think this is the case but it would be worth making sure.

Something I talk about a lot with students is how they can come up with something like the above structure when they are under pressure and when the case question is something they've never considered before.

There are a number of things that can work – not all will work all the time of course.

First of all, you need to use your common sense and business judgment. You are a clever person who is naturally interested in business (why else would you be at University or Business school?). You also have a lifetime of experience of reading the news, hearing about businesses doing things such as launching products and entering markets etc. Finally, as a consumer/customer/patient you have been involved in a great many businesses.

So hopefully when you hear a question about a common issue such as entering a new market, or launching a product, or buying a competitor, this is not the first time in your life you have encountered such an issue.

In addition to your prior experience, you will perhaps have done a practice case already about this issue – this is where getting a good volume of cases under your belt can really help. The more you've done, the greater the chances that you've already considered such a question.

The thing you have to train yourself to do, even if you have read many business articles and thought very frequently about the issue before, is to frame the issue in the key points – to structure it.

Listen to your inner voice – the answer that pops into your mind is often a good place to start - I often find that when I hear a question, one of the first things that pops into my mind is a potential answer. For instance, if you asked me if an American burger chain should launch in India, I might instantly assume that it would be a bad idea because I don't think there is a big demand for burgers in India (I may be very wrong on this).

If this happens to you, the trick to learn is how to hold that thought in your head, and then ask yourself – **is this a high level category or is it a detail?**

If it is a detail, ask yourself two questions – **what kind of category would this fit into, and what other details would fit into this category?**

Let's apply that to this example

First we have our thought:

Do Indian consumers have a strong demand for American burgers?

Question: is this a high level category or is it a detail?

Answer – I think this is a detail

Question - what kind of category would this fit into?

Answer – something about consumer demand. Perhaps I could phrase it as 'is there a market for this product?'

Question - what other details would fit into this category?

Answer – Hmmm... tricky because right now I'm stuck on the idea of a burger restaurant with nobody in it. But if I push myself (especially if I allow myself the possibility of coming up with something out of the box or even wrong) to investigate the question of 'is there a market for this product?' I might also come up with:

- Is there a market in India for fast food? (what type – sit down restaurant or take-out/drive-through)
- Is there a market for our non-burger offerings?
- If there isn't a market for beef burgers could we come up with local alternative or equivalent?

You could go through the above sequence on paper – you could write out the case question at the left hand side, then when you think of your potential answer you could write that on the right hands side, then go through the exercise of filling out the middle row (categories) then going back to the right hand side for the other details in that category.

Once you've done that category, ask yourself the next question: What else should this company think about, apart from whether there is a market there?

Another way to phrase this question is: **Assuming I've answered my first category** (in this case, there IS a market) — **is the case question answered, or is there anything else we should think about?**

You can use this approach to build up a good set of categories.

Even if my very first thought was a detail, I often find that once I've got a category on the page, I can look at that and come up with another category. Remember, for each 'level' of thinking (or things of equal hierarchy in a tree), the things should be roughly equivalent in scale. So if my first category is 'Is there a market?', I can't come up with a second category titled 'Does the client have any staff who have experience in India?'. This feels too much like a detail, so I have to push myself to be more comprehensive, and come up with a category along the lines of 'Does the client have the capabilities to execute this expansion?'

If I had written the 'staff with experience in India' question as a category, I should have then looked at it, realized my mistake, and moved it. This method of iterating your structure is perfectly acceptable — it is great for the interviewer to be able to see your thought process.

While we're talking about structure, I think we should mention MECE

MECE is an acronym apparently invented by McKinsey. It stands for Mutually Exclusive and Collectively Exhaustive.

MECE is a guideline, not a rule!

Mutually Exclusive is a good way to think about your categories. It would be a very messy structure if each category had big overlaps. But in practice, life is complicated, there WILL be overlaps. Let's say the answer to 'are there any regulatory hurdles' is yes. There might be an answer in there about hiring somebody who is an expert in working closely with the Indian Government to get a license. Does that point go in the category about regulation, or does it go with Internal Capabilities? Probably both.

Nevertheless, Mutually Exclusive is a good high level goal as you are drawing out your structure.

Collectively Exhaustive is another good guideline, but absolutely not the goal in the truest sense of the word. Why? Collectively Exhaustive does not sit well with getting to an answer quickly. If you wanted to examine absolutely every element of whether there is a market for burgers in India you might spend weeks or months on the internet, on the ground, interviewing consumers, reading research reports, getting to a very detailed answer. You don't have time for this in a 20 minute case interview. So your goal is a lot more like 'Have I covered the most important drivers' rather than 'Have I exhausted every possibility?'

Why can't I just memorize a bunch of existing structures?
Think back through what we've just been talking about. A case interview is a bit like an audition to see how you think through a new problem, and whether you have the ability to summarize the ways you would approach such a problem.

It is not a situation where the interviewer is looking to see if you have memorized an existing answer.

Let's be clear on this. It is not like an exam where you are cramming a certain number of absolute facts that you can then regurgitate on demand.

Another way of putting this - If you were asked the question about going into India as a burger restaurant and you leapt up and said 'Wow, that's freaky, my previous job was as head of strategy at an American burger chain and I had to answer exactly that question, so let me tell you, here's what we looked at and here's the answer!'. Do you think the interviewer is going to run back to the decision room and say 'Hey guys we can call off the search, we finally found the guy who knows the answer – let's hire him so that if we ever have to deal with this case we've got the answer waiting!!'

Of course not. The interviewer is not earnestly seeking the answer. He is looking to see how you handle something you haven't thought of before.

What happens frequently is that the interviewee pulls out a memorized structure, that in this case is not 100% right. Perhaps it contains a category that for this question is simply not an important driver, or perhaps the language used shows clearly that this is a structure that would better suit a different business. This shows that not only have you memorized a framework, but that you are not clever or intellectually nimble enough to realize that your memorized framework is not the right one to use. Don't get yourself into this situation.

Here's an example.

Let's say I asked you a different version of the same question. I've come up to Tuck to interview you, and Tuck is located in the small rural town of Hanover, New Hampshire. I'm a Tuck alum and you are a student, so we both know the town well.

'I'm thinking of opening an Indian restaurant on Main Street in Hanover. Is this a good idea?'

You think to yourself 'great – this is very similar to that practice case I did about launching a burger chain in India, I'll re-use that framework', so you say to me'

"OK, great, I'll want to think about the market, the competitor landscape, the client capabilities, and the regulatory landscape."

This sounds to me like a pre-prepared market entry strategy. I was looking for something a lot more like:

"Oh wow, that would be interesting, I've often wondered why there isn't an Indian restaurant on Main Street, especially when you think of how many Indian students there are at Tuck, and also how many restaurants of other nationalities there are in Hanover. Let's look at that

— I'd probably want to test that thought about how many students and local residents in Hanover would be interested in Indian cuisine. I'd also want to look at what's already out there... I know Yama does really well with its Korean menu for instance, as well as all the traditional American restaurants like Mollies and the Canoe Club. I'd want to talk with you about your expertise in the restaurant business, and whether you intend to run it yourself or hire a manager, and finally I'd want to learn about how the town of Hanover regulates the use of buildings on Main Street."

If you think back through this section on structure, we've gone through a journey. We started with a question we hadn't thought of before, we came up with a way for you to answer that question live, and to come up with a useful structure. In that initial structure, especially in the details, we had a lot of tailored content that used the language of the case. It probably wasn't perfect, and there are probably other ways you could approach that question, but it showed the interviewer that you can attack a new question, go through the process, and come up with a structure.

That process is what you need to go through, live, in front of the interviewer, each time you do an interview. Even if you've done exactly that question as a practice (it can happen), you need to put yourself through that thinking process again, and let the interviewer see you go through it. In particular, assuming you haven't done this exact question before, you need to ensure that you answer the specific question, not an approximation of it that you have practiced for. Keep the memorized generic framework in the back of your mind, and use it when you are brainstorming content, but don't let it slip out.

How do I know whether I should lead the case or not?

Sometimes the interviewer will guide you through the case. Sometimes this will be very clear, the interviewer may interrupt you and move you on to the next 'task'. McKinsey case interviews are often like this. On the other end of the spectrum, you may get an interviewer who gives you the initial question, then sits there with folded arms, silently, expecting you to lead the whole discussion.

So how do you know which interview you are in?

Firstly, it will probably be pretty clear to you by the way the interviewer acts.

Secondly, the safest bet is to assume that you will be leading the case. It shows that you are the kind of person who likes to drive things, who is comfortable taking control of a conversation.

How do you lead a case?

Think back to your structure. If you've done it right, you've created a roadmap for yourself – a set of questions and topics that you need to go through in order to be able to answer the question. So leading the case should now just be a matter of methodically working through your structure, gathering answers, and coming to a conclusion.

In practice, the interviewer will very often have planned to spend more time on a particular category than on others. If this is the case she will guide you that way. Sometimes she will look at your structure and tell you that one of your categories is not relevant, or she will quickly give you the answer to it. Other times she may allow you to start exploring, but her answers will be high level and she will not give you detail, and from this you should infer that there is not a rich discussion to be had.

How should you ask for data?

Consultants love data, and so should you as an aspiring consultant. Very often a category or a detail can only be answered by examining some form of data. For instance, if we are determining the market, we might explore a data table that shows the current data on numbers of people in India in each major city who regularly eat out at fast food restaurants.

Sometimes the interviewer has an exhibit to give you, and sometimes they have memorized data. Other times they don't have it at all.

We've already covered the fact that you shouldn't get into the trap of thinking of a case as a treasure hunt, where you are seeking the 'code word' that will unlock the data exhibit. You should instead think like the owner of the problem, following through your roadmap, and asking for information where you want it. Err on the side of asking yourself at each detail – what kind of data could I ask for that might prove or disprove, or in some way answer my question. Tell the interviewer what you are thinking, why you want the information, and ask if they have it.

How do you know when you've finished?

Sometimes even a strong candidate will get to the end of their exploration, when they have answered all of the things they set out to answer, and will then look at me expectantly, and then ask "Is there anything else you wanted me to talk about?"

You are in control. You are the detective. You set out your roadmap at the beginning and you have been leading the discussion.

When you have finished answering all of the questions you set out to answer, and you now have the answer you set out to find, you are ready to conclude.

You could launch into your summary, or if you wanted to play it safe, you could use some kind of language that lets me know you are about to conclude. That way, if there really was something else I wanted us to cover, you have at least given me as the interviewer a chance to stop you and direct you on to the remaining point.

You could say something like:

"Looking back at my initial structure, I think we've covered all of the questions I set out to answer, and these answers allow me to make an overall recommendation, therefore...

By now, if I wanted to stop you, I could have jumped in. Otherwise, you should go ahead and make your recommendation/summary/conclusion, which, as we all know, should be concise and answer-first.

How can I improve my public math?

When you're given a math problem, or when you encounter a part of the case where a calculation is going to provide you with useful insight, you are being tested on a few different things:

1. Are you comfortable with numbers?
2. Can you set up your calculation in a logical manner?
3. Can you do the computation?

Actually, the first point is the most important. The interviewer is looking at you very closely as you get those numbers, so think carefully about how you react, what your body language is showing, and what you say. Get into the habit, if you are handed a data exhibit, of saying 'Great!', and remembering to smile and nod enthusiastically. It sounds obvious, but you'd be amazed at how many people, on being given some data or a math puzzle, literally sigh deeply and shake their head.

Setting up the calculation is a trick I was taught when I first studied case interviews as an MBA student. I'm about average (for an MBA) at math – I've got the basic skills, but I certainly don't practice them on a daily basis, and it is many many years since I've done arithmetic without using a calculator or computer.

The advice I got was to lay out the calculation in logical steps, and then talk through the logic, before leaping in to the actual numbers. This is similar to the way that students in Excel modeling are taught how to approach building a model – before you touch the computer, you should have drafted a good plan that shows what you are aiming to calculate and how you'll calculate it. If you get this step right, even if you get one of the interim calculations wrong, you will probably be OK.

Doing the computation is a matter of working through it. It's absolutely OK to do it on paper. Remember how to do long division? If not, you need to brush up. When you are doing the calculation, be methodical – show that you take this seriously. When you have your answer, sense check it to see if you are in the right ballpark. Be particularly careful when you are working with large numbers and lots of zeros, or if you have at some point changed scale (i.e. from thousands to millions).

As I said, when I was doing this it had been a long time since I'd done mental arithmetic, or even done arithmetic on paper. You're probably in a similar situation. So this should be something you take seriously as a learning goal – by the time you walk into the interview you need to be back in shape.

How can you get back to the teenage math whiz that hopefully you once were?

There are a great many websites that have math puzzles you can do – you could focus on case interview prep sites, or GMAT prep sites, or you could broaden your approach to the kinds of math sites that a twelve year old might be using (seriously!).

Get in the habit between now and the interview of making yourself do calculations in your head or on paper. Set yourself math questions. Compare the prices of different products in a store. Calculate the tip. Calculate the tip if it was 7%, or 17% (not just 10% or 20%!). Work out how fast you'll get home if you continue to drive at the current speed. Work out how much longer it would take you if you drove 10mph slower. Divide the journey into three chunks, assume three different speeds, for 3 different lengths of road, and calculate an overall weighted average (interviewers love giving you weighted averages).

I remember I bought a book on tricks and tips for mental arithmetic. I can't remember any of those tricks now, but for the couple of months when I was prepping for case interviews, they really helped me get back in the zone of feeling like I was good with numbers.

Whatever it takes, and however you choose to do it, you need to get yourself to the place where you feel like you are great with numbers, and you are happy to do calculations on paper and in your head. If you get to that happy place, it'll show through in the interview. If not, you'll be one of the people who is sighing, shaking your head and literally putting your head in your hands. Don't be that person!

How can I improve my creative thinking?

The ability to come up with creative, new and unexpected ideas is valued in a consultant. Where would this come into play in the day to day job? Most often during a team meeting where everyone in the room is pushing themselves to ensure they have thought of every eventuality (just as you are doing when you are creating your structure). It also comes into play when you are counseling a client who has of course thought of all the obvious answers, but has brought you in to give a fresh perspective.

I often found that my most creative, and useful, ideas came when I took a break from the computer screen, got up from the desk, and actually thought about something else (or thought about nothing at all). It's a cliché but it's true that very often the brain does its best processing when it is not being pushed, hence the number of great ideas that come when you are in the shower, or driving to work, or even asleep.

Clearly a case interview is a long way from being asleep, or in the shower. Your brain is actively focused on the task at hand, and this is not always the most conducive atmosphere for creative, or out of the box, thinking. So how can you get yourself into the creative zone under interview conditions?

Here are some techniques that may help:

Use analogies:

Let's say you're doing a healthcare case, and are thinking about ways to get obese patients to take up a new exercise regimen. You've put down everything that came into your mind, and the interviewer is still asking 'what else'?

You could pick an example of a product that you know well, and think about the way that it is marketed. Perhaps that leads you to some interesting ideas. Or you could think of other circumstances where people are persuaded to do something that is for their own good, but where there is reluctance to overcome. Wearing seatbelts? Quit smoking? Floss?

You may not always come up with any more ideas, but even the fact that you show that you are willing to try an analogy would get you credit.

Give yourself permission to fail:

Sometimes the block to your creativity is your own censor. You are being interviewed for a job where intellect and common sense are valued, and you don't want to make yourself look foolish by coming up with wrong ideas. That's understandable.

If you are trying to be creative, and push the boundaries, sometimes you are going to come up with things that aren't great ideas.

So you could try saying something like "I think I've got all the main ideas here, but I want to brainstorm to see if I can come up with anything else", or "I'm not an expert in this industry, so some of the ideas may be off the mark, but I'll try to think outside of the box..."

Imagine yourself in the situation:

Try putting yourself into the picture – if you are discussing grocery sales in a supermarket, imagine yourself as a customer, pushing a shopping cart around the store. Imagine yourself as a variety of different types of consumer, an elderly shopper who isn't very mobile, a parent with a couple of toddlers, someone who is new to the store and is rushing around looking for what they need. Sometimes these 'role plays' can throw up some interesting nuances, and again they show the interviewer that you are earnestly seeking as many ways of deriving insight as possible.

Keep asking why:

'5 Whys' is a powerful technique for getting to the heart of an issue, and can be useful in a case for really getting below the surface. Let's say you've come up with a hypothesis that the problem with profit margin in a superstore is that the manager has recently reduced the price of a low margin line of goods, and thus the sales mix has skewed towards this low margin item. It's easy to lean back at this point and think 'great! I've solved the case!', but you'll get extra credit if you take a minute to ask 'why would the manager have done that?' Perhaps the manager is incentivized to grow same store sales (i.e. revenue, not profit). Why is that? Perhaps the CEO has promised a certain same store sales figure to investors. Why did she do that? Perhaps a competitor is aggressively publicizing its successful same store sales growth. If you went through this quick brainstorming exercise, you might come up with some useful insights that would direct you to a far richer solution than simply 'fix the pricing of the low margin item'.

What is an 'answer-first' summary?

When it comes to the end of the case, it is the convention that there is usually an opportunity for you to give a brief summary. Often the wording goes something like this: "The CEO or consulting partner has just walked into the team room and asked you for the answer – what do you tell her?"

Clearly the interviewer doesn't actually need a summary of everything you have discussed for the last half hour – they have been in the room with you! What they are looking for is a demonstration of a few key skills:

They want to see that you can communicate efficiently

They also want to see that you can speak confidently.

After having a fairly broad discussion for only a short amount of time, your natural response when being asked to give a summary is to let the interviewer know how many questions you still have that haven't yet been robustly answered. Of course, a real consulting engagement would last longer than half an hour. This is one of those parts of the case which is slightly different from reality. So the way to approach it is to assume that you have been through the whole case, and to imagine that you really are in the position where you can make a final recommendation.

Often I'll do a practice case with someone and ask for their recommendation, and they'll give me a summary of what we have discussed, ending with the answer. My feedback to them in this case is that they should practice being **answer-first**.

Laying out the evidence, then the conclusion, is the classic way of telling a story. It's what leads to the satisfying bit at the end of the book or TV episode where all the parts of the story are tied together. If it is a detective story there will be an 'aha!' moment where the criminal and his methods are revealed. Because this is how most of our stories go, this is how we most naturally tell them, even in business. There are indeed some situations in business where this is also required. For instance, if you knew that your answer was going to be difficult for the client to accept, you may lay out the evidence first, ensure they agree, and then make the conclusion.

In the case interview, however, you want to treat the script as you'd write a PowerPoint page, or a newspaper article. You'd start with the headline (the answer).

Using our burger restaurant example, the summary might be:

"**You should enter the Indian fast food market**. You should do this by launching a chain of restaurants that sells American style burgers tailored to local tastes. As we've seen, there is a clear market demand, and the only current competitors are small scale local companies. We have the management bandwidth, although you should seek a leader for this venture who has some experience in India – this would need to be an external hire."

When you've finished, stop talking. Really. It's natural to continue to add another layer of detail. Then another. Avoid that urge.

I've got the basics, but what are they *really* looking for?

As I said at the start of this book, with my analogy of racing drivers, a consulting company is not just looking for someone who can competently do the basics, they are looking for a star performer. So what makes the difference between competently 'cracking the case' and actually getting the job? What are they REALLY looking for?

First, let's just take a second to absorb the fact that 'acing', 'cracking', 'nailing' or 'solving' the case is not going to get you the job all by itself.

Think back to the criteria that I suggested you use when analyzing a case:

- Ability to plan a structure
- Use of common sense, business acumen and creativity
- Ability to do the numbers
- Feels like a consultant

Most of them are to a certain extent technical. You need to come up with a structure, you need to demonstrate your mathematical ability, you need to show you can use creativity and business knowledge. All of these could be done by a computer or a robot. But the consulting company is not looking to hire a robot. The element that we haven't yet covered is the slightly more amorphous one – 'do you feel like a consultant?'

Feeling like a consultant means that from the second you walked into the building, or picked up the phone, to the second you left, you acted in a manner that made all those who met you think that if they hired you today, and you showed up for work tomorrow, you'd be able to walk straight into a client meeting and act in a way that would represent you and the firm well.

Elements that go into this include:

- Confident, yet not arrogant
- Professional demeanor
- Friendly
- Enjoying solving the problem
- Trustworthy

I don't believe that anyone reading this lacks the above traits. I do believe, however, that in a stressful interview situation, many people don't allow the above traits to show.

So how can you accentuate the traits that make you 'feel like a consultant'?

The biggest issue is confidence. You are walking into a once in a lifetime interview with one of the most selective companies in the World. It's natural to be nervous. And logically the people interviewing you should realize that. After all, they were all once in the same situation. The problem is, people tend to make emotional judgments such as this based on what they see in front of them, so it's up to you to hide that nervousness and come across as friendly and confident. If this sounds unfair, think of it this way – if you get the job, there will definitely be times you have to walk into a stressful meeting with a senior client and you will need to use the same skills then.

There are a number of ways you can boost the appearance of self-confidence on the day of the interview.

If you are somebody who gets jittery, and really needs to calm down, try meditating or simply working through some breathing exercises.

If you are somebody, like me, who very often gets quiet and withdrawn when stressed, you need to 'pump yourself up'. Exercise is a great way to do this. I spoke recently with a student who said that he often gets the feedback that he is too quiet in an interview, but that for the job he ended up getting he'd had to do a 30 minute walk across the city to get to the interview – by the time he got there his adrenaline was going, and he was physically 'pumped up'. This is a great technique. If you are staying in a hotel, perhaps get into the stairwell and walk up and down the stairs for five minutes. Or do some pushups in your room. Whatever it takes to get your heart working (but not too much that you arrive sweaty and out of breath!)

If there are any doubts in your mind that you are the best candidate for this job, you need to put those doubts away. Think about the times in your life when you have been absolutely at the top of your game. Perhaps it was in a sporting setting when you or your team just won. Perhaps it was a time when you achieved something really difficult. Think carefully about that time. Remind yourself of how you felt like you could do no wrong – like you were 'in the zone'. The more details you can remember about that time, the better.

Finally, you can also focus on the outward signs of confidence. Let's call this the 'fake it 'til you make it' strategy. Even if you are so nervous you want to throw up, and so sure of your upcoming failure that you almost canceled the interview, there are still some pieces of 'acting' that might help you through.

Smile. Smile a lot. Before you go into the building spend a minute doing some massively exaggerated smiles, just to get your smile muscles warmed up. As you walk up to the receptionist or greeter, remind yourself to smile. As you meet your interviewer – you get the idea by now – smile.

Use lots of positive words. As you're going through the interview, remind yourself to say things like 'Fantastic', 'Great', 'That's really interesting', 'Wow', 'Fascinating' etc.

Finally – never give up. There may be a time during the case when you feel like you haven't done your best. Perhaps you've made a math mistake, or you realize you missed a key part of the structure. Don't give up. Very often such mistakes are not terminal. The interviewer knows you are under pressure, and has probably seen a lot of diversity of performance. If you can admit your mistake, 'keep calm and carry on', very often the interviewer will give you another chance.

What is the difference between a first and second round interview?

Some companies have material differences between first and second round interviews. Perhaps they will do a traditional case in the first round, then a group case in round two. I'm not going to list out all of the companies and all of their plans – they will give you that information when you need it.

What I'm talking about here is the fact that even when both first and second round (and beyond if there are more rounds) use traditional case interviews, there is sometimes a different feel or style, such that a person who felt well prepared for round one might feel unprepared for round two.

Essentially the differences that you may experience are as follows:

- First round interviews are more likely to be conducted by a relatively junior consultant, and second round interviews are more likely to be conducted by a more senior consultant, probably a manager or partner.
- First round interviews are often checking that you meet the basic standards. The question in the interviewers mind is 'should I put this person through for a further interview? Decision round interviews are clearly a step further, where the question at the decision meeting is 'shall we give this person a job?'
- First round interviews can sometimes be on your 'home turf' – perhaps by phone, perhaps on your campus. Final round interviews are very often on the firms' 'turf'.

People quite often feel that they were well prepared for round one, but that round two threw them off their game. That's because most of their practice was with peers, testing the basics, in a known location. Don't underestimate the difference in feel it can make when you step up a gear to a senior interviewer, who is probing you beyond the basics of the case, in their office.

There is another reason why the case that a partner gives you may feel different from that given by a junior consultant – their style has simply evolved over time. Imagine a situation where a group of people get trained in a way of doing things. After that initial training, they do the activity in a situation where none of their peers gets to see them do it. They do it reasonably frequently for a long period of time. Let's say you checked in on them after 10 years. You're probably going to see some considerable variance in style. We can probably assume that a junior consultant, who was trained in interviewing recently, will do it in the style in which he or she was trained. A senior partner, on the other hand, may think they are doing it in the style in which they were trained but that training may have been a long time ago. They may also have made a conscious choice to change their style (after all, when you're a partner at a consulting company, you get used to making your own rules!)

Why was the partner rude to me?

Slightly different from the circumstance described above, where the partner may have a different style of giving a case, there is also the fact that sometimes a more senior interviewer actually has a different goal from the interview. They can assume that the early round of interviews tested the basics, but now they want to test something different. They want to test how the interviewee responds to pressure, and they also want to test whether the interviewee can handle being challenged by authority.

This can lead to what for many people becomes a very uncomfortable interview. In fact, very often interviewees after such an interview will say that the partner had been mean or rude to them.

So was the partner being rude, and if so why?

One of the great things about consulting companies is that they value the intellect and creativity of their employees. They use this intellect and creativity in a number of ways, and one of the most powerful is by putting a number of them into a team and letting the team debate an issue. This may be at an early stage, where the debate is about the big picture, or it may be towards the end of a project, where the debate is more about the details of the solution. Either way, when the team is gathered in such a meeting, every team member will be expected to give their opinion, with little or no regard for seniority.

So if I'm a partner, and I am conducting a decision-round interview, **I want to find out if you are the kind of person who will contribute to a discussion, even when there are senior people present**. I might choose to do this by pushing back on some of your ideas during the case. I may purposely disagree with you. I might even use fairly abrupt language. What I'm looking for is the type of person who likes being intellectually challenged in this way – the type of person who likes a debate. Don't get me wrong, I'm not looking for someone who gets aggressive or who defends every idea they've ever had – if my idea is genuinely better I want you to consider it and agree if relevant, but I want to see that you like being challenged.

I am also very aware that some of my clients can be fairly abrasive, and do not treat junior consultants well. So **I want to find out if you can remain professional (polite, calm, and thoughtful) when you are being challenged.** Again, I might use the case interview as a way to treat you in a way that I would not naturally treat you as a colleague. Some of these ways might verge on the theatrical. For instance, I may ignore you and stare out of the window. I may take a phone call while you are talking. I may play with my iPhone. I may continually interrupt you. Many of the above are in some way a simulation of what it's like to be meeting with a client who doesn't value your contribution. Many of these situations can be won by a person who has good skills at communicating and influencing, whereas they would be turned even worse by someone who gets either too quiet or too aggressive in such a situation. Therefore, despite the fact that the interview itself may be uncomfortable, it is a pretty good opportunity for you to showcase your skills.

To conclude, if it appears that the interviewer is being rude to you, it is very probably for a reason. They are probably testing you to see how you react, and what they are looking for is someone who remains professional, does not get visibly stressed, actually seems to like being intellectually challenged, and in an ideal scenario can 'win over' a difficult client.

'Fit' interviews

Case interviews get a lot of air time amongst people trying to get a consulting job, but most firms will also have a certain amount of fit interview – the type where they seek to find out if you'd fit well with the work they do, and the culture of their firm.

In this section, we'll look at the following issues, all of which frequently come up during recruiting season:

- How much weight does the fit interview have compared to the case? (If I nail the case, am I assured of the job?)
- What are they looking for?
- I've heard that company X doesn't do fit interviews, how do they get people that fit with their firm?
- I'm very good at talking about myself, so do I need to practice?
- Should all my stories be from professional experience?
- How recent should my stories be?
- Can I duplicate stories between interviews?
- What curveball questions might I get asked? (And why?)
- Will they be seeking to test me on industry or functional knowledge?
- Will they ask who else I'm interviewing with?
- Is there any kind of general preparation I can do?

How much weight does the fit interview have compared to the case? (If I nail the case, am I assured of the job?)

If you take away nothing else from this chapter, please consider this one point:

An excellent performance in the case interview alone is not enough to get you the job.

Assuming that a company will have some portion of their interview process devoted to fit (even if it's just a few questions about your resume on the way into the room), then you can be sure that you will need to pass that part of the interview just as impressively.

Why is it important to know this?

If you really admit the above fact to yourself, then it should have an impact on the way you prepare for your interview, and definitely should have an impact on the way you allocate your prep time.

Too often I see candidates who devote 95% of their prep time and energy to case practice. Along the way they assure me that they are going to practice 'fit stuff' "as soon as they're comfortable that they are ready with cases. This is a natural reaction to being given a new and challenging task (learning case interviews) alongside what seems like a relatively easy task (talking about yourself in a fit interview).

Here's my opinion on the importance of the fit interview. I'll express it numerically so there can be no doubt.

I think that a hiring decision is based on about 40% case performance and 60% fit performance.

You can debate with me about the numbers all you want (should it be 51/49 or 80/20), but what you should take away from this is that the fit interview component is MORE IMPORTANT than the case.

So perhaps you should think again about how you will assign your prep time.

Counter intuitively, I would even say that the less confident you are about your consulting interview skills, the more emphasis you should put on fit prep. If you get a number wrong on a calculation, but I love your fit stories, I will be fairly likely to say to myself "hey, it's only natural to get nervous and make a simple math mistake, but I really want this person on my team so I'll hire them anyway." Conversely, if I don't feel like you'd fit in well with my team, or represent my firm well in front of an important client, I really don't care how well you did in the case, I'm not going to hire you.

What are they looking for?

Consulting companies are looking for a number of personal attributes, or competencies. These competencies do not really vary from firm to firm, although some may place slightly different emphasis on different areas.

McKinsey, for instance, publishes the following key competencies that it looks for in candidates:

- Problem Solving
- Achieving
- Personal Impact
- Leadership

Therefore, you can reasonably expect the fit interview to seek to understand how you might be judged along the above criteria.

All companies will have similar characteristics that they are looking for. During the interview they will be listening out for evidence that you fit the bill.

There are a number of ways that they can test for these characteristics. The most common is to ask you to tell a story about a time when you…

(insert evidence of characteristic here). What I mean by that is if I want to find someone who has a natural strength in achieving, I might ask a questions along the lines of "Tell me about a time when you achieved something difficult." This could actually be phrased many ways – here are some different questions which all seek to get to the fact that you are somebody who values achievement:

- Tell me about something you are really proud of.
- Tell me about a time you had a really difficult task ahead of you.
- Tell me about something really difficult that you chose to do.
- Tell me about the most challenging thing you've ever faced.
- What's your greatest achievement?

I've heard that company X doesn't do fit interviews, how do they get people that fit with their firm?

I was once having lunch with a senior partner at one of the top firms. As part of her job she also looks after MBA recruiting. I'd attended a recent seminar given by some consultants from her firm, where they talked about interviewing. They'd stated that students shouldn't expect any 'fit' component in their interviews – just case. Yet this was a firm that is renowned for hiring people who 'fit' with its culture.

I asked the partner how they achieved their goal of hiring people who 'fit' the culture of the firm, without doing any 'fit' interviewing.

The partner gave me the kind of look that made me realize I'd asked a silly question, and replied "Surely you realize that it's ALL a fit interview." What I took her to mean by this is – "While you're doing mental gymnastics with your math and structure, what we're really looking for is the 'soft' stuff – how well you are building a relationship with the interviewer, how comfortable you are under pressure, how driven you are to succeed, etc.

I'm very good at talking about myself, so do I really need to practice?

People don't actually say this to me, but I know they are thinking it. The usual scenario is this: Interviews are a few weeks away, they have already spent a couple of months on intensive case interview practice, and they have come to me for another practice. I ask them when they are going to stop doing case practice and start working on their fit stories. They look at me like I've just suggested they need to go and practice tying their shoelaces.

Please believe me when I say that the fit interview is every bit as worth practicing as the case interview. And if I think of all the many hundreds of people I've helped get jobs at top consulting companies, many of those who really moved the needle did it by focusing on their fit stories.

Think about the experience of watching a really well-written TV show or play, or reading a great novel. Do you think that stuff was made up on the spot? Do you think you're experiencing the result of the first draft? No, it was drafted, re-drafted, re-written, polished, edited, rehearsed, polished, and re-written a huge number of times.

I'm not suggesting that you need a Hollywood script editor and a whole room of writers in your corner, but you can certainly borrow from their techniques.

Here's my advice.

Let's take the example of the question "Tell me about something you're really proud of".

First of all, stop and think about what the interviewer is trying to get at. What kind of boxes are they hoping to check?

Here's my suggested list. You could probably improve it.

- Sets difficult goals / Motivated to achieve
- Comes up with sensible ways to approach a difficult task

- Is not discouraged by set-backs
- Can learn from experience, and changes course when required
- Draws on help from others when required. If so, is able to influence and lead.
- Is introspective – able to think carefully about own experience.
- Is able to communicate well – draws me into the story

Writing this kind of checklist is a great way to keep you on track.

The next step is to think of a story from your past experience that could answer the question and satisfy the recruiter's curiosity about the above points.

Write out the story in note form, now read it through.

Many people when they write out, or tell, such a story will find that they have the following structure:

Situation (50%)

Your life is complicated. So are the challenges you face. Therefore you probably have to give me quite a lot of context so that I can really understand it.

Task and Action (10%)

You've heard of the Star Model (Situation, Task, Action, Resolution), but really Task and Action tend to blend together. They don't take too long because we want to get to the outcomes.

Resolution (40%)

Here's what happened when you solved the problem. The result is something you are proud of and you've heard that recruiters like you to drive to results.

Example:

Here's a truncated version of a story that I could tell from my past.

Before I decided to come to B school I worked in television for about ten years. I had studied film and TV at university, and after that I got a job as part of a TV crew making a series for the Discovery Channel. This was great fun, and a true learning experience. Eventually I teamed up with a friend to found a TV production company. We won some commissions from a UK TV channel and threw ourselves into building that company. But at the back of my mind was always the fact that I'd entered the industry with the ultimate goal of making a feature film. I really wanted to stand on set as the director of a movie, and one day walk into a movie theater that was showing my film.

So I set myself the goal of making a feature film, which involved raising money – my co producers and I raised about $150,000 in cash investment and convinced most of the cast and crew to defer their salaries, which was equivalent to a total production cost of around one million dollars.

The film got made, and I got to live my dream of being a director. We didn't get a theatrical release, but we did sell the DVD rights to Warner Brothers, which I'm very proud of.

So what's wrong with this structure?

The problem with spending a lot of time on context and setup is that it is not really answering any of the questions the recruiter is seeking to answer. Of course you can't dive in without any context, but do your best to limit this.

What's wrong with spending a lot of time on results? Actually results are not at all interesting to the recruiter. This is counter-intuitive. You may think that the fact that you achieved 4x revenues for your company is a big deal, and perhaps on your resume it makes a nice bullet point, but it doesn't tell me much about the questions I'm seeking to answer.

Here's what I'm REALLY listening out for:

- How hard was the thing you had to do?

- After knowing how hard it was, what were you thinking?
- How did you plan to do it?
- Why did you choose that plan?
- When you started working through the plan, what went wrong?
- With any people you dealt with, did they always agree with you or did you have to influence them in any way?
- What was your darkest hour? (the time you were most tempted to quit)
- What did you learn by doing this?
- What would you do differently if you did it again?

The structure should look something like this:

Situation (10%)

Task (including making the plans, thinking about how to influence people etc.) (40%)

Action (40%)

Results (10%)

Here is the structure applied to my example.

Before B school I worked in TV, where I had my own production company, but I'd always wanted to make a feature film. There were a number of problems with that goal though. In terms of the scale, in any particular year in the UK probably about twenty films get made, even though many thousands of projects are in development. Films are expensive to make, and usually only experienced producers and directors get to make them. And in terms of money, I certainly didn't have any of my own money to invest, and couldn't see a way to get financial backing. Also I was a TV guy, and most TV guys are not seen as film guys.

But I was absolutely determined to succeed, because this was my dream, and had been since I'd been a kid. So first of all I did a lot of research, talked to everyone I knew in the industry, and found out that sometimes films get made even though they don't have an ultimate customer yet. Most of these get made quite cheaply because the cast and crew agree to defer their salary until such a time that the film makes money. The difficulty with this is you need to get about 100 people (cast and crew) to agree to work for you for essentially no pay, doing a job that is very arduous. My team worked 6 days a week for about 12 hours a day for about 5 weeks. That's a lot to ask!

The other thing I found was that I had incredible support from my colleagues and friends. Once I'd set the vision of making the film, and got them excited about the idea, they really pitched in and if it weren't for them it wouldn't have happened. It's funny because I hadn't really thought of myself as a 'leader' before that, but it was really the fact that I stepped forward, and said "I'm doing this, who's with me?" that made the whole thing happen.

So eventually I did raise enough money and get enough people to work with me, and it did happen. We didn't manage to sell it for cinema release, but it is available on DVD, and I'm incredibly proud of the achievement.

So this above version is what I'd consider a reasonable first draft. But there's still room for improvement.

A common area for final touches is to add more colorful detail. Think of a great movie or novel. As well as the broad strokes of the story, there are countless details that stick with you forever. Often these are very minor things like the way a room looked, or the words that someone said.

On interview day, your interviewer may be seeing ten or more people. At the end of the day she will have to go into the decision room and defend her decision to hire you to the rest of her team. Make it easy for her by providing memorable details, or 'sound bites'.

Here are a few suggestions:

Help me 'see' it.

Did your work take place in a gleaming office building where glass walls meant everyone could see you even when you were engaged in stressful phone calls? Did you have to walk down onto the shop floor and talk with the shop foreman during his lunch break, while the rest of the crew sat and watched your conversations? Were you launching your start-up from a small, dusty office that you had to share with another entrepreneur who insisted on filling the space with his own product samples? Did your potential investor ask to meet you in a hotel restaurant where everything was so expensive you could only afford the cheapest thing on the menu?

Give me details like the above, and they'll stick with me.

Get down to the real 'crunch' moments.

For many tough things in life, there are moments where you really hit rock bottom, or made a crucial decision. Slow down the narrative and spend some time on that point.

Here's one from my example:

Day two of filming was meant to be on set, where the art department had spent about a week constructing a set of a room. Every time I checked in with them during that week of set-up they'd promised me it would be ready in time, but I was doubtful. When I checked in on them at about 5am on the day of the shoot, it was clear to me that it wasn't good enough. I felt sick. I couldn't delay the shoot, and I knew that if we used the set then the whole movie would be ruined. Yet if on day 2 I told the art department that their work wasn't good enough (even though they were working for nothing) they'd probably quit. I remember walking outside, and my co-producer came up to me, and he could see from the look on my face that things weren't good. We sat and talked it through and came up with an action plan...

Get inside the heads of those around you

You always get bonus points for showing how good you are at understanding others, and ideally using that understanding to influence them in some way. So if there was a point where somebody was in your way, or was disagreeing with you, then show me that you knew what they were thinking, and why they were thinking that, and more importantly how you used that understanding to come up with your own plan to influence them.

Be reflective

Your story doesn't have to be an unmitigated success story. It's very compelling sometimes if you can pause and admit that looking back you would have done things differently. It shows that you are thoughtful, honest, and able to learn from your experience. The flipside of this is someone going through a story which is so impossibly successful and well told that it sounds unreal – like a used car salesman giving a pitch.

Should all my stories be from professional experience?
Use your judgment. You should present the best story for the circumstance. If that story is from personal life, then go for it.

One possible exception is if you are a 'non-traditional' candidate about whom the recruiter might already have some doubts about your business experience. For instance, you might be a former professional athlete, or a doctor, or a military veteran. In these cases, you will undoubtedly have many strengths that 'traditional' candidates could not even dream of, but there will be a certain doubt about how you will perform in the 'real world'. If you fall into this set, and you are presented with an opportunity to either use a 'business' story or a personal one, you might want to err on the side of business.

How recent should my stories be?
Again, there is no fixed rule here. Generally you should be using stories from your adult life. That can include University. Clearly if you have had

15 years of work experience since then, you would probably not reach that far back.

For me it depends on the strength of the story. If you climbed Mount Everest or won an Olympic gold medal when you were 18 years old, you might still draw on that story. But in that case I would still make sure that the rest of your stories were more recent and 'real-World'.

Can I duplicate stories between interviews?

You can re-use a story on different days. Therefore if you have a first round set of interviews on campus and then are invited to final rounds in an office, you could re-use your stories in the office round.

On the other hand, within any of the above days, or if all of your interviews are compressed into one day (what some firms call a 'power round), then you cannot repeat the story.

Imagine the scenario – your interviewer excitedly bursts into the decision room and says "I met this great candidate who had to overcome considerable odds to start her own space flight business!". The other interviewers agree that you were great, but all have the same story from you. The result will be disappointment for them, and for you. They need a variety of experiences to make sure that you are not a 'one-trick pony'.

What curveball questions might I get asked? (And why)

This goes back to what we covered in the Case Interview chapter ("Why was the partner rude to me?"). Sometimes you might get questions that are a deliberate attempt to set you off guard.

Sometimes when I am interviewing somebody, I will get the feeling that all of their answers are too rehearsed. The good thing about rehearsed answers is that it shows me you have taken the interview seriously and prepared accordingly. The bad thing is that I don't really get a sense for you and how you think. So in that case I might respond by deliberately choosing a question that is uncommon, just to see how you react. If you are very polished and confident, I might push you to tell me about your weaknesses, or a failure, to see if you are a well-rounded individual who can admit that everything has not always gone your way.

Particularly with Business School students, I might want to get beyond the kind of business thinking that you have picked up in the classroom. I might ask you about recent trends in my industry to see if you are the kind of intellectually curious person who keeps up to date on business news. I might ask you what the most interesting article was that you read recently. I might ask you what your favorite company is, and why you like it.

A senior partner at a top consulting company told me that his favorite question is to ask "If you think about your most recent/current job, what would you do to improve that company?" He said that answering this well shows you are somebody who is always thinking about how to do things differently.

A student a couple of years ago was asked "Which of your brothers and sisters is your favorite?" Clearly the interviewer in this case is not going to make a hiring decision based on which sibling was the favorite. Most likely this was another attempt to see how the student could handle a challenging question. An appropriate response might be something like "That's a crazy question! I couldn't possibly choose!", said with a smile on your face that shows you are happy to be challenged in such a way.

Will they be seeking to test me on industry or functional knowledge?

If you are interviewing for a generalist consulting position, it is unlikely that you will get pushed very far for knowledge of a specific industry. Of course, any industry that you have worked in is fair game, and you should expect to be up to date on recent stories from any industry and company on your resume.

If you are interviewing for a particular industry or functional practice, or indeed if you are interviewing with a company that has such a focus, you can expect to be tested on your expertise.

Will they ask who else I'm interviewing with?

This is a fair question for them to ask. Sometimes you have an answer that makes you seem desirable, for instance if you are also interviewing with other top firms. Even better, if you have an offer already from someone else, let them know. Interviewing someone who you know already has an offer elsewhere feels different.

If you are not interviewing with anyone else, you could make a virtue of that fact, although an answer of "No, McKinsey is the only company I'm interested in", flattering though it is to McKinsey, risks making you seem like somebody who is not well able to judge risk. Something like "I'm interviewing with a number of firms" is probably safer, and is what they'd expect to hear.

Is there any kind of general preparation I can do?

Write out all of the competencies you think the company is looking for. For each of these competencies, think of at least two stories from your past that demonstrate you have exactly that competence. Ideally each story would also touch on some or all of the other competencies. Write out either in full or in bullet form your stories. Practice saying them out loud. Practice with other people. Practice a lot.

Do your homework on the company you are interviewing with. Make sure you are familiar with materials that are on their website. If you have spoken with anyone from the company during your recruiting process so far, remember their names, and be prepared to talk about them.

Keep up to date with business news. This is difficult if you are busy studying. I get it – I was there. But the strong candidates will distinguish themselves not just by cracking the case but by being able to talk knowledgably about current affairs. And have opinions. If there is a major story at the time, have an opinion on it.

Remember it's all a fit interview! Even when you're plugging away at the data in a case interview, remember they're looking for someone who likes challenges and is great at making relationships, so look up from the paper, smile, and show that you are having a good time!!

Managing Offers

Congratulations! You made it through the process and you just got a phone call from the partner at your dream firm, making you an offer. Let's assume you didn't give an answer on the phone (they won't be expecting you to) and that they said they'd get the paperwork to you in due course.

First of all, pop open the champagne, go out and celebrate! Everything else can wait a day or so.

So what's ahead of you?

If you are at business school, going through the process with a major firm, there may well be a 'sell weekend' coming up, where the firm will bring all of its 'offerees' to a nice location where they can wine and dine, and try to convince you to accept the offer.

The firm may set up a long list of phone meetings for you to speak with current consultants, all of whom can sing the praises of the firm.

You might get gifts sent to you. In a good season this might be a valuable haul. In a lean season it might be nothing.

Overall, it's a great time, and you should enjoy it.

But what if you then get another call, from another one of your dream companies? Now you're in a great situation (you have more than one offer) that can actually turn out to be quite difficult and uncomfortable.

1. Firstly, the sell weekends of competing companies may clash.
2. Secondly, once the firms find out (perhaps you'll tell them, or perhaps word will get back to them via another student) that you have another offer, their phone calls will intensify
3. Thirdly, perhaps you really don't have a strong feel for which firm would be best for you

Firstly, don't worry. You are not being ungrateful, it can be genuinely stressful to be in this situation.

If you want to, there is nothing wrong with saying to a company that you have enough information; you just want some time to think, and to request them not to set up any more phone calls for you.

It is OK to only attend half of a sell weekend if you want to split the weekend across companies (if this is feasible)

It is OK to make a decision based on whatever criteria you want to use.

The main thing is to be honest with all firms at all times. If there is an offer you know absolutely you will not accept, you should let the company know as soon as possible. If you have said yes to a firm, you should tell all other firms immediately and stop recruiting.

Final note

Thanks for buying my book, and for sticking with it! I hope you will find it a useful step on your career journey.

One of the many things I learnt from being a consultant is that feedback, if sometimes painful to receive, is always useful.

In that spirit, if you have feedback, suggestions or comments on ways this book could be improved, please do let me know – you can email me directly at Stephen.pidgeon@tuck.dartmouth.edu

Finally, if you have enjoyed this book (or for that matter if you haven't!), please consider writing a review on Amazon. I personally find honest reviews incredibly valuable when I am considering any kind of purchase.

Thanks!

Stephen

Hanover, NH

Summer 2015

About the Author

Stephen Pidgeon is Associate Director in the Career Development Office at the Tuck School of Business at Dartmouth College, which is consistently ranked amongst the world's top business schools. In his role at Tuck, Stephen helps students get internships and full time positions in all of the world's top consulting companies; including McKinsey & Company, Bain & Company, The Boston Consulting Group, Deloitte Consulting, and many more. Each year, Stephen coaches hundreds of MBA and undergrad students, helping them navigate the on-campus recruiting process, and coaching them to succeed in consulting case and experience interviews.

In addition, Stephen is one of the most sought-after interview coaches on Evisors.com, where he coaches students (including undergrad, MBA and other advanced degrees) and experienced hires.

Prior to working at Tuck, Stephen was an Engagement Manager at McKinsey & Company, based in the London office, during which time he served top leaders of many global organizations. He was particularly active as an interviewer, attending company presentations on campuses, mentoring candidates, and taking part in countless interviews and decision meetings.

Stephen received his MBA from the Tuck School of Business in 2007, where he successfully navigated the consulting recruiting process, receiving offers from two of the top consulting firms. He spent his summer internship with McKinsey & Company.

Stephen lives in Vermont with his wife and two daughters, and when he is not writing or coaching students spends his time renovating his house.